# Options Trading Workbook for Beginners

# What are Options?

Options are a contract that gives a person the option to buy or sell an option within a specified period of time at a specified price. The minimum number of shares in a contract is 100; so the person has the option to buy or sell a 100 shares minimum.

For example, James wants to buy Apple stock. Apple stock is currently at $100. In a traditional investment, James could buy as many stocks as he wants at $100/share. Let's say he decides to buy 50 shares. He spends $5000 to buy 50 shares.

If James were doing an options contract, he would retain the option to buy a minimum of 100 shares of Apple (1 contract) within a specified period of time at a particular price.

If James buys 1 contract that expires in 6 months and he has locked in a price of $100. He paid $30 for the contract. The $30 is called the premium for the contract.

That means, he has the option to buy Apple stocks for $100 regardless of the actual price of Apple stock. So, if Apple is at $150 after 4 months, he can buy at $100 per share and profit $50 per share (or $50*100=$5000 per contract).

James can also sell options to other buyers if he owns 100 shares of Apple. James gets the premium and the buyers get the option of buying the stock from James.

Options can sometimes be less risky than buying the stock as James only spends $30 for the contract instead of buying 100 shares of Apple for $10,000.

## How It's Used

Options are a great addition to an investor's toolkit, and are used in several ways to enhance a person's portfolio:

1. **Buying time to decide whether to buy a stock**

If you're unsure about whether to buy a stock and you want more time to decide, you can buy an options contract to buy the stock within a specified period of time. This gives you additional time to decide whether you want to buy before the expiration of the contract.

2. **Leveraging cash to increase purchasing**

One of the benefits of options trading is that the premium of the options contract costs a lot lower than actually purchasing the stock.

So, you can buy several options contracts for the price of the actual stock. This lets you magnify your gains if the stock rises by the expiration date.

### 3. Hedging against a stock market crash

Another options strategy is to purchase the option to sell stock that you own at a specified price (put option). So, if you own 100 shares of a stock you can buy the option to sell it at a particular price within the expiration date of the contract.

So, if the stock crashes way below the price you cap the downside risk by selling it a higher price than the actual price (after the crash).

This lets you improve your odds in the stock market when there is a crash.

### 4. Sell Options and Get Passive Income

You can sell options and collect premiums from buyers.

If you select the right strike price, premiums, and time periods; this can be a reliable source of income.

This does require a bit of expertise to consistently get premiums while making sure that you don't lose money due to the contract being executed by the buyer.

Some of these terms may be confusing for now, but it will make sense when we describe them later in the book.

Problems with Traditional Options Trading Strategies

1. **Taxes**

Options trading gains are treated as short term capital gains tax so a significant portion of it is taxed at the highest rate based on your income bracket.

2. **Commissions**

Most brokers charge high commissions for options trades, further reducing the profit.

3. **Requires monitoring of positions and expertise**

Options are a great way to generate extra income, and hedge against market volatility; but it requires a lot of knowledge and practice to implement correctly.

However, implementing the wrong strategies at the wrong times can have the opposite effect; and you could lose more than you ever could in the stock market.


In this book, we are going to include tons of options in worksheet form, so you can practice hypothetical situations; and learn about the benefits of options.

We will also look at a couple of situations that you should definitely avoid due to the high risk involved.

While taxes and commissions do eat into your profits; keep in mind that the income you derive from options is an extra side income. So, the extra income will come as a great benefit even though it is mitigated through taxes and commissions.

# Options Trading Terms and Definitions

## Call Option

A call option is a contract between a buyer and a seller.

The seller of the contract owns at least 100 shares (1 contract) of a stock.

The buyer has the option to buy the stocks from a seller at a specified price within a specified time.

The buyer pays the seller a premium for the options contract.

Here's a simple example below:

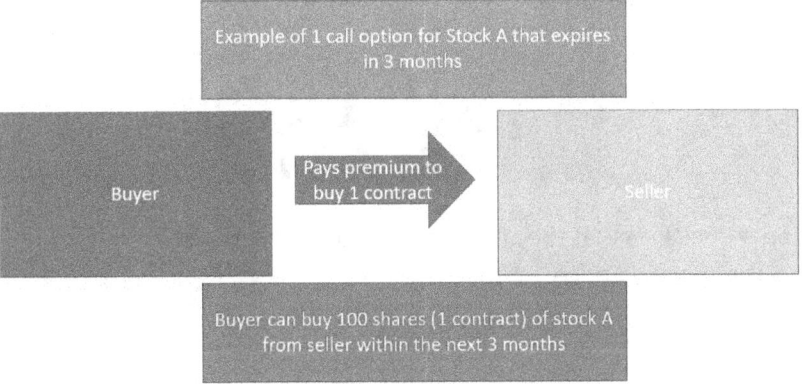

The buyer believes that the stock will go up in the specified time period.

## Put Option

A put option is a contract between a buyer and a seller.

The buyer may own at least 100 shares (1 contract) of a stock.

The buyer has the option to sell the stock to the seller at a particular price within a specified period of time.

The buyer pays the seller a premium for the option.

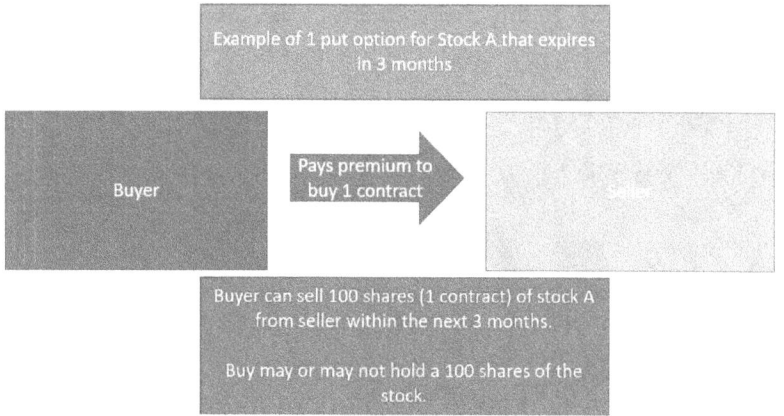

The buyer believes that the stock may go down in the specified time period below the specified price.

## Strike Price
Strike Price is the specified price at which a call or put option is executed.

## Expiration Date
Expiration date is the date at which the call or put option expires.

## Premium
Premium is the amount that the buyer of the option pays to the seller.

# Options Chain with Example

An options chain is a list of all available options contracts for a particular security (stock).

Below is an example of an options chain for the stock Southern Copper (ticker symbol SCCO):

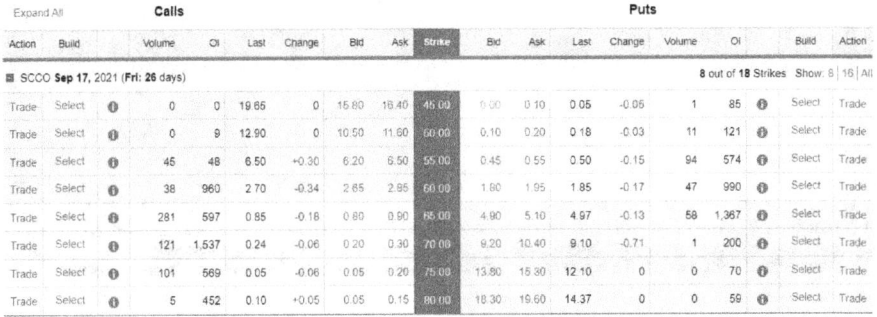

Source: Charles Schwab

The options expire on September 17th, 2021.

The middle column of the chain (highlighted in dark blue) is the strike price.

On the LH side of the strike price are all the call options for each strike price.

On the RH side of the strike price are all the put options for each strike price.

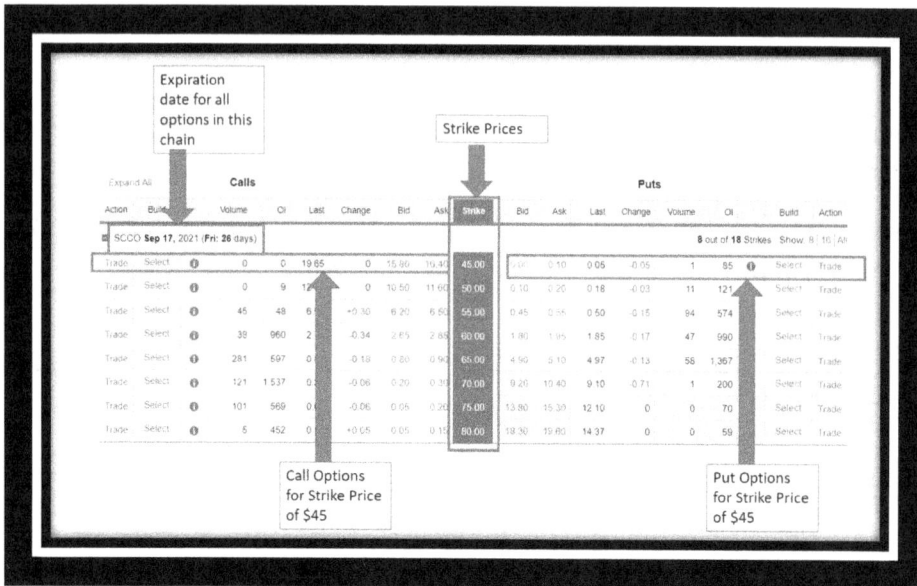

Now, let's have a look at a particular line on the chain. We're picking out the call option for strike price of $45.

The premium of the option is between $15.8 and $16.4 per share. So, purchasing a contract would cost between $1580 and $1640 (for 100 shares).

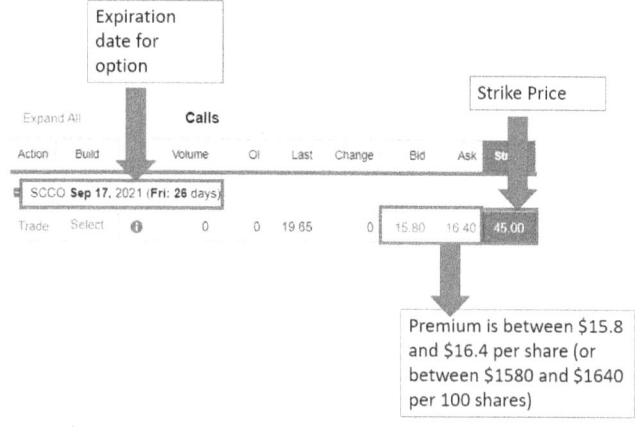

Now, let's look at the same put option on the chain for a strike price of $45.

The option costs between 0 and $0.1 per share (or between $0 and $10 per contract).

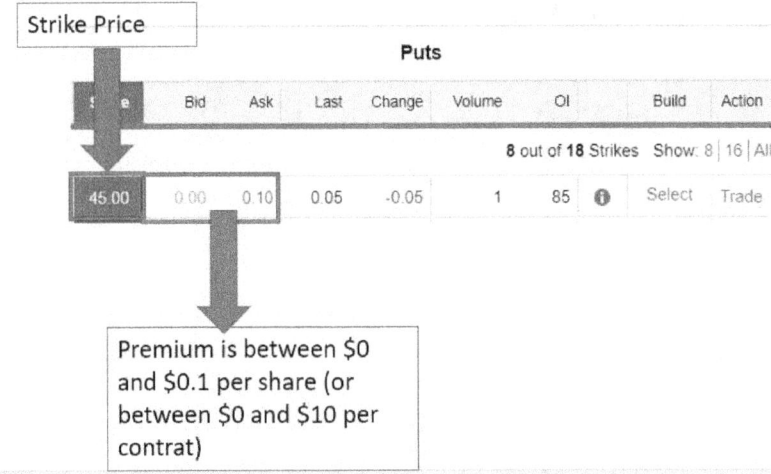

Why is the $45 put option so much cheaper than the call option?

This is because the current price of the stock is $60.79. It is much higher than the strike price of $45; which drives up the demand for the $45 call option. The high demand drives up the price of the call option.

However, the $45 put option is cheaper because it is unlikely that the stock is going to fall below $45 by September 17th, 2021 (in 26 days).

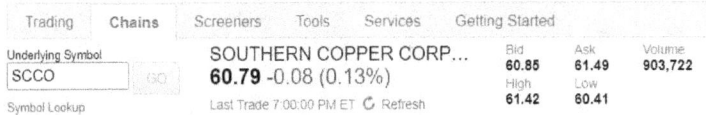

# 5 Practice Options Chains

Now, let's revise a few options chains. All the terms in this chapter will be explored in detail later. For now, it's important that you can identify the different elements to move forward.

## Chain 1

Source: Charles Schwab

a. What is the stock involved in the Options Chain?
b. What is the current price of the stock?
c. What is the expiry date of the option?
d. What is the cost range of the $70 call option?
e. What is the cost range of the $80 put option?

# Chain 1 (Answers)

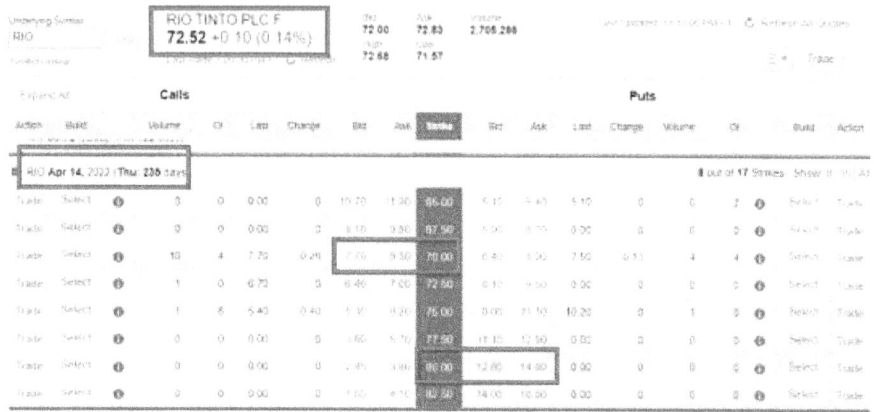

Source: Charles Schwab

a. What is the stock involved in the Options Chain? **RIO Tinto (RIO)**
b. What is the current price of the stock? **$72.52**
c. What is the expiry date of the option? **April 14, 2022**
d. What is the cost range of the $70 call option contract? **$770-$850**
e. What is the cost range of the $80 put option contract? **$1280-$1480**

# Chain 2

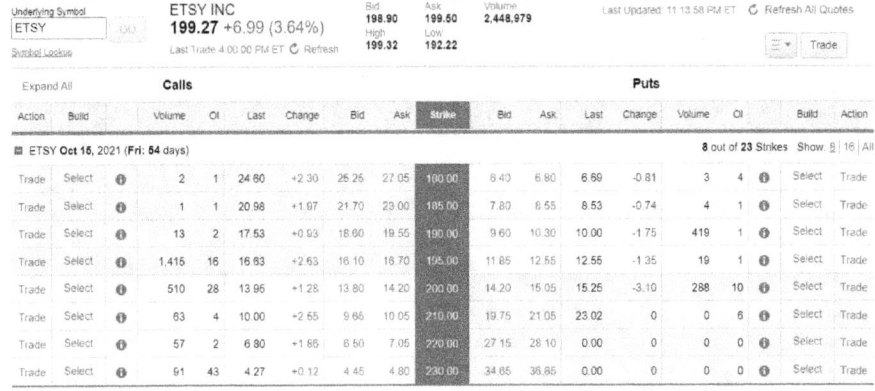

Source: Charles Schwab

a. What is the stock involved in the Options Chain?
b. What is the current price of the stock?
c. What is the expiry date of the option?
d. What is the cost range of the $180 put option contract?
e. What is the cost range of the $200 call option contract?

# Chain 2 (Answers)

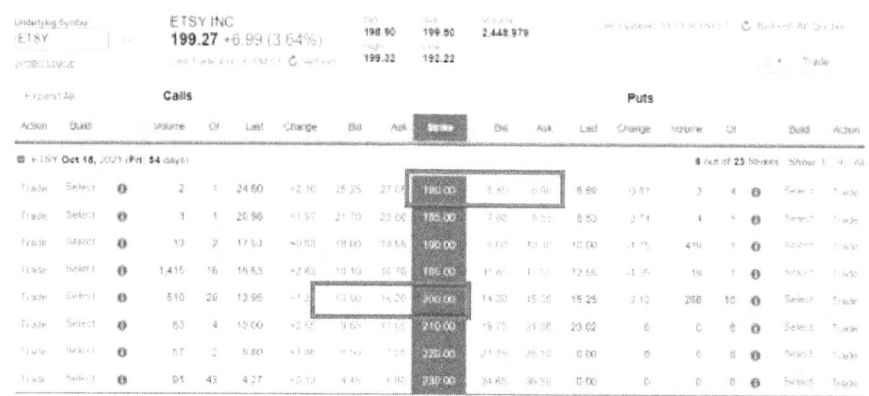

Source: Charles Schwab

a. What is the stock involved in the Options Chain? **ETSY INC (ETSY)**
b. What is the current price of the stock? **$199.27**
c. What is the expiry date of the option? **October 15, 2021**
d. What is the cost range of the $180 put option contract? **$640-$680**
e. What is the cost range of the $200 call option contract? **$1360-$1410**

# Chain 3

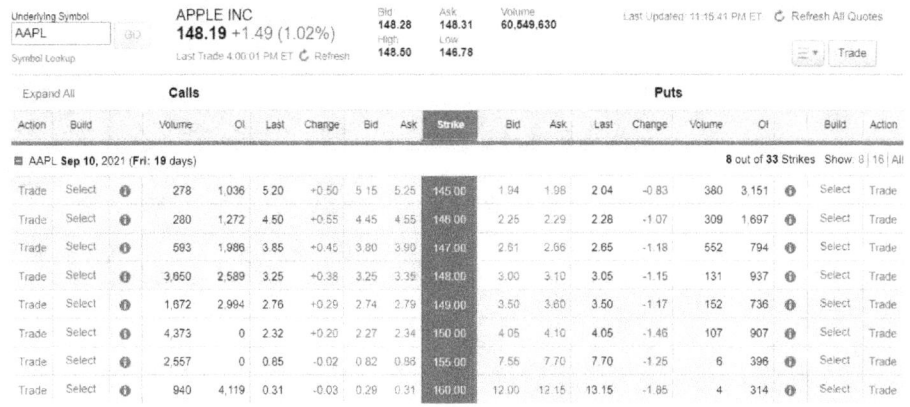

Source: Charles Schwab

a. What is the stock involved in the Options Chain?
b. What is the current price of the stock?
c. What is the expiry date of the option?
d. What is the cost range of the $150 put option contract?
e. What is the cost range of the $145 call option contract?

# Chain 3 (Answers)

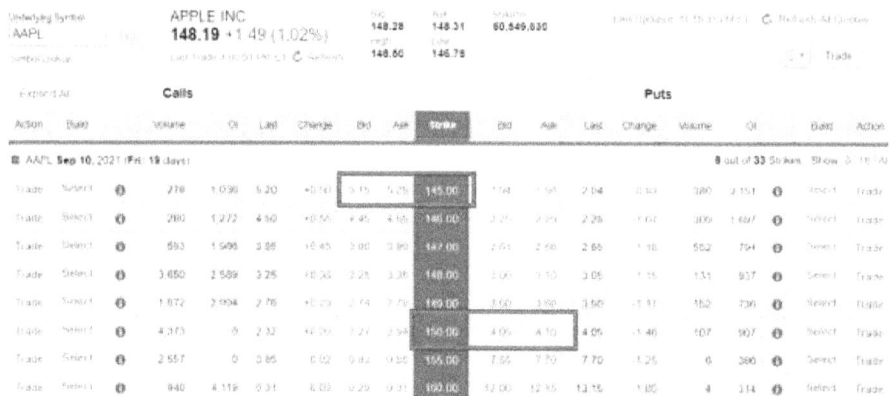

Source: Charles Schwab

a. What is the stock involved in the Options Chain? **APPLE INC (AAPL)**
b. What is the current price of the stock? **$148.19**
c. What is the expiry date of the option? **September 10, 2022**
d. What is the cost range of the $150 put option contract? **$405-$410**
e. What is the cost range of the $145 call option contract? **$515-$525**

# Chain 4

Source: Charles Schwab

a. What is the stock involved in the Options Chain?
b. What is the current price of the stock?
c. What is the expiry date of the option?
d. What is the cost range of the $340 put option contract?
e. What is the cost range of the $330 call option contract?

## Chain 4 (Answers)

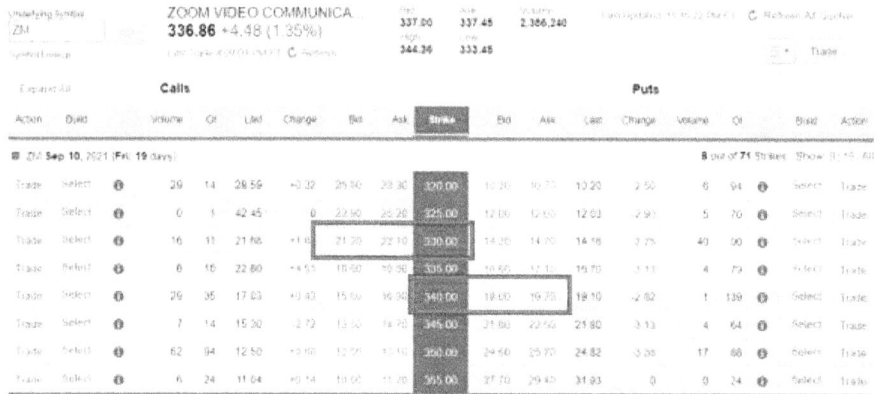

Source: Charles Schwab

a. What is the stock involved in the Options Chain? **ZOOM VIDEO (ZM)**
b. What is the current price of the stock? **$336.86**
c. What is the expiry date of the option? **September 10, 2021**
d. What is the cost range of the $340 put option contract? **$1900-$1970**
e. What is the cost range of the $330 call option contract? **$2120-$2210**

## Chain 5

| | | Calls | | | | | | | Puts | | | | | | |
|---|---|---|---|---|---|---|---|---|---|---|---|---|---|---|---|
| Action | Build | Volume | OI | Last | Change | Bid | Ask | Strike | Bid | Ask | Last | Change | Volume | OI | Build | Action |

FB Sep 17, 2021 (Fri: 26 days) — 8 out of 87 Strikes Show: 8 | 16 | All

| Action | Build | | Volume | OI | Last | Change | Bid | Ask | Strike | Bid | Ask | Last | Change | Volume | OI | | Build | Action |
|---|---|---|---|---|---|---|---|---|---|---|---|---|---|---|---|---|---|---|
| Trade | Select | ⓘ | 60 | 5,464 | 22.90 | +2.61 | 22.60 | 22.85 | 340.00 | 3.25 | 3.40 | 3.25 | -1.67 | 438 | 6,299 | ⓘ | Select | Trade |
| Trade | Select | ⓘ | 76 | 2,782 | 18.70 | +2.10 | 18.55 | 18.80 | 345.00 | 4.25 | 4.40 | 4.23 | -2.22 | 164 | 2,816 | ⓘ | Select | Trade |
| Trade | Select | ⓘ | 471 | 32,487 | 15.10 | +1.93 | 14.95 | 15.05 | 350.00 | 5.55 | 5.65 | 5.48 | -2.57 | 629 | 6,936 | ⓘ | Select | Trade |
| Trade | Select | ⓘ | 700 | 3,509 | 11.65 | +1.65 | 11.60 | 11.80 | 355.00 | 7.20 | 7.35 | 7.15 | -3.03 | 385 | 2,571 | ⓘ | Select | Trade |
| Trade | Select | ⓘ | 1,877 | 7,608 | 8.75 | +1.25 | 8.70 | 8.85 | 360.00 | 9.30 | 9.45 | 9.10 | -3.69 | 198 | 4,838 | ⓘ | Select | Trade |
| Trade | Select | ⓘ | 1,335 | 4,289 | 6.37 | +0.90 | 6.30 | 6.45 | 365.00 | 11.90 | 12.10 | 11.95 | -2.92 | 156 | 4,652 | ⓘ | Select | Trade |
| Trade | Select | ⓘ | 497 | 29,013 | 4.51 | +0.41 | 4.45 | 4.55 | 370.00 | 14.95 | 15.20 | 14.72 | -3.43 | 25 | 1,262 | ⓘ | Select | Trade |
| Trade | Select | ⓘ | 502 | 7,170 | 3.15 | +0.31 | 3.00 | 3.15 | 375.00 | 18.55 | 18.80 | 19.01 | -4.06 | 9 | 628 | ⓘ | Select | Trade |

Source: Charles Schwab

a. What is the stock involved in the Options Chain?
b. What is the current price of the stock?
c. What is the expiry date of the option?
d. What is the cost range of the $340 put option contract?
e. What is the cost range of the $330 call option contract?

# Chain 5 (Answers)

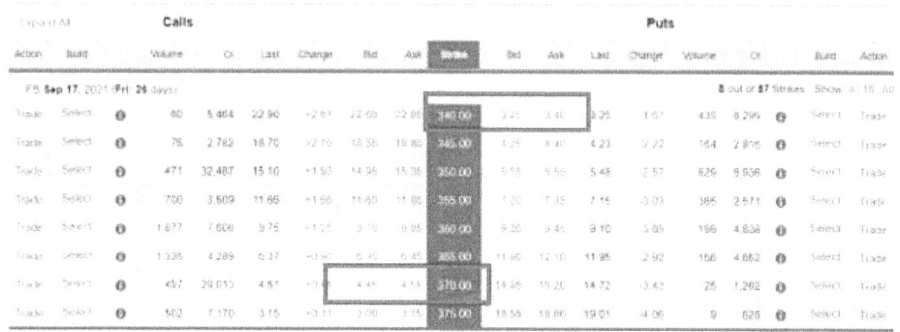

Source: Charles Schwab

a. What is the stock involved in the Options Chain? **FB**
b. What is the expiry date of the option? **September 17, 2021**
c. What is the cost range of the $340 put option contract? **$325-$340**
d. What is the cost range of the $370 call option contract? **$445-$455**

# Buying Calls

So far, we've touched on the basics of options trading and options chains. In this chapter, we will go into more details about buying calls.

## Psychology behind buying call options

Let's say you've been investing in the stock market for a few years. You've been buying stocks with the hope that it goes up. It seems like a safe way to invest your money. Stocks generally go up with inflation. The Dow Jones has gone up for the last 100 years.

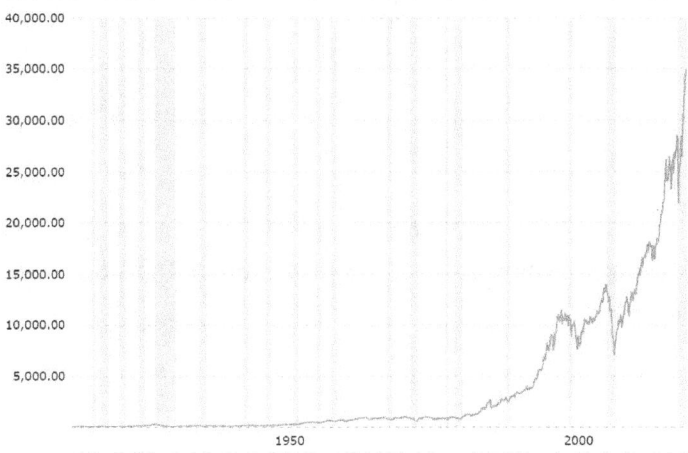

Source: Macrotrends

What could go wrong? Well, plenty….

If you're investing in a broad index fund, keep in mind that there have been several periods in history where the stock market has had negative returns for periods of 20 years or so.

Let's look at the Dow Jones from 1930-1950 below.

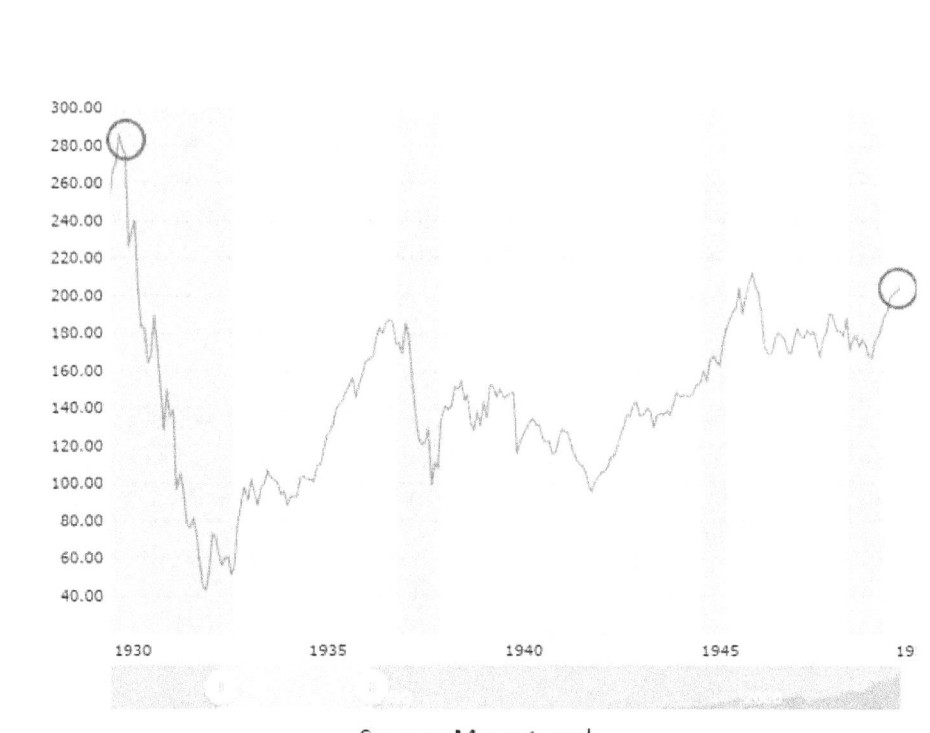

Source: Macrotrends

If you invested $1000 in the Dow Jones in 1930, it would be worth $720 in 1950. That's a negative return over a 20-year period. The stock market always goes up, huh??

Let's look at another example. Here's a chart of the Dow Jones between 1965-1980.

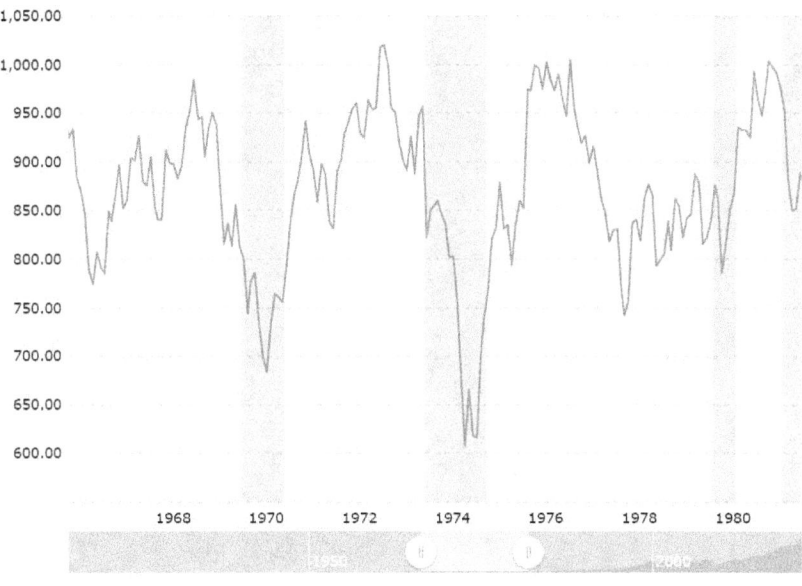

Source: Macrotrends

If you invested $1000 in 1965, it would be worth $900 in 1980. A negative return over a 15-year period?? And you know what's crazier?

This was during the 1970's stagflation era, where the inflation rate was 6.8%.

This means that you would have lost 67% of your purchasing power had you invested in the Dow Jones.

And let's look at a final example. Below is a chart of the Japanese stock market between 1990 and 2020. If you had invested a $1000 in 1990, you would have $700 in 2020.

Source: Macrotrends

These 3 examples show the importance of picking quality stocks and risk mitigation in your stock portfolio.

While filtering through quality stocks is an art in itself, that is not the objective of this book.

We are going to focus on risk mitigation using Options trading. Buying call options is one strategy that you can employ.

# How Buying Call Options Work – An Example

So, let's have a look at a simple example of how buying call options work.

We're going to buy 1 contract of ETSY stock. The options chain is below.

We're going to buy 1 contract of ETSY at a strike price of **$200** that expires in 54 days (on October 15, 2021).

We pay a premium of between $1380 and $1420 for the option to buy 100 shares. Let's say we pay **$1400**.

So, let's look at what happens after 54 days (at contract expiration). Let's look at three different scenarios.

### Scenario 1: ETSY is at $210 per share.

You have the option to buy 100 shares of ETSY at $200.

So, you would have a gain of $210-$200=**$10 per share.**

So, you gain a profit of $10*100=**$1000**

However, remember that you paid $1400 for the premium.

So, Loss = $1400-$1000 = **$400 Loss**


**Scenario 2: ETSY is at $250 per share.**

You have the option to buy 100 shares of ETSY at $200.

So, you would have a gain of $250-$200=**$50 per share.**

So, you gain a profit of $50*100=**$5000**

However, remember that you paid $1400 for the premium.

So, Profit = $5000-$1400 = **$3600**


**Scenario 3: ETSY is at $190 per share.**

You have the option to buy 100 shares of ETSY at $200.

However, since ETSY is below $200, it makes no sense to exercise the contract and buy the shares.

So, you lose nothing on the 100 shares.

However, remember that you paid $1400 for the premium.

So, Loss = **$1400**


So, your maximum loss if **$1400** no matter how low the stock goes. This caps your downside.

You start making a profit once the stock goes above **$214** and there is no cap on your profit.

This is shown in the chart below:

## Call Options vs Buying a Stock

So, the main benefit of buying call options is that you don't have to buy the stock. You buy an option to buy the stock. You can exercise this option at any time before expiration. This reduces your downside risk, as you only lose the premium for the option instead of the entire money invested in the stock. The cost of the premium is a lot lower than the cost of buying the stock.

Now, let's look at an example. Buy Tom and Jim have $400 money to invest in NAT stock

Tom buys 150 shares of NAT stock, while Jim wants to buy 5 options contracts of NAT.

The current stock price is $2.30.

Below is the options chain.

| | | Calls | | | | | | | | Puts | | | | | | |
|---|---|---|---|---|---|---|---|---|---|---|---|---|---|---|---|---|
| Action | Build | Volume | OI | Last | Change | Bid | Ask | Strike | Bid | Ask | Last | Change | Volume | OI | | Build | Action |

NAT Apr 14, 2022 (Thu: 233 days)                                                                                                   8 out of 10 Strikes Show 5 | 15 | All

| Trade | Select | 0 | 0 | 0.00 | 0 | 0.01 | 4.80 | 0.50 | | 2.14 | 0.00 | 0 | 0 | 0 | Select | Trade |
| Trade | Select | 0 | 0 | 0.00 | 0 | | 3.50 | 1.00 | | 2.19 | 0.00 | 0 | 0 | 0 | Select | Trade |
| Trade | Select | 0 | 25 | 1.50 | 0 | | 3.10 | 1.50 | | 2.29 | 0.00 | 0 | 0 | 0 | Select | Trade |
| Trade | Select | 0 | 0 | 0.00 | 0 | 0.05 | 2.78 | 2.00 | | 4.60 | 0.00 | 0 | 0 | 0 | Select | Trade |
| Trade | Select | 0 | 0 | 0.35 | 0 | | 2.53 | 2.50 | | 2.68 | 0.00 | 0 | 0 | 0 | Select | Trade |
| Trade | Select | 0 | 1 | 0.46 | 0 | 0.15 | 0.50 | 3.00 | | 3.10 | 0.00 | 0 | 0 | 0 | Select | Trade |
| Trade | Select | 0 | 0 | 0.00 | 0 | 0.07 | 2.36 | 3.50 | 0.05 | 3.55 | 0.00 | 0 | 0 | 0 | Select | Trade |
| Trade | Select | 0 | 0 | 0.00 | 0 | | 2.30 | 4.00 | 0.05 | 4.80 | 0.00 | 0 | 0 | 0 | Select | Trade |

NAT Jan 20, 2023 (Fri: 514 days)

Tom spends $2.3*150 shares=**$345**

Jim decides to buy 5 contracts of NAT which expires in 233 days (on April 14, 2022). The premium is between $5 and $270 per contract.

| Trade | Select | 0 | | 0 | 0 | 0.00 | | 0 | 0.05 | 2.78 | **2.00** |

Let's say Jim pays a premium of $50 per contract. So, he spends a total of $50*5=**$250** for 5 contracts.

So, let's look at what happens after 233 days (at contract expiration). Let's look at three different scenarios.

**Scenario 1: NAT is at $0.5 per share**

Tim's market value of 150 shares = 150*$0.5 = $75

Tim's Profit = $75-$345=-$270 = **$270 Loss**

Jim has the option to buy 500 shares at $2 per share. However, since the value of the stock is below $2, it makes no sense to buy the stock. Jim loses nothing on the value of the stock.

However, Jim paid $250 for the contract.

Jim's Profit = -$250 = **$250 Loss**


**Scenario 2: NAT is at $3 per share**

Tim's market value of 150 shares = 150*$3 = $450

Tim's Profit = $450-$345=+**$105 Profit**


Jim has the option to buy 500 shares at $2 per share. So, Jim buys 500 shares at $2 and makes a gain on the different between market value and current value.

Jim's Gain = 500*$3 – 500*$2 = +$500

However, Jim paid $250 for the contract.

Jim's Profit = $500-$250 = +**$250 Profit**


**Scenario 3: NAT is at $5 per share**

Tim's market value of 150 shares = 150*$5 = $700

Tim's Profit = $750-$345=+**$405 Profit**


Jim has the option to buy 500 shares at $2 per share. So, Jim buys 500 shares at $2 and makes a gain on the different between market value and current value.

Jim's Gain = 500*$5 – 500*$2 = +$1500

However, Jim paid $250 for the contract.

Jim's Profit = $1500-$250 = +**$1250 Profit**

|  | Scenario 1 | Scenario 2 | Scenario 3 |
| --- | --- | --- | --- |
| Tim (Buys Stock) | -$270 | $105 | $405 |
| Jim (Call Option) | -$250 | $250 | $1250 |
|  |  |  |  |

Jim comes up better in all 3 situations. Of course, this would depend heavily on the premium paid for the stock.

If you have the same amount to invest in call options vs buying a stock, it is definitely a good idea to investigate buying a call option.

# Call Options Worksheet

# Call Option 1

| | | | | | | | | | | | | | | | | | | |
|---|---|---|---|---|---|---|---|---|---|---|---|---|---|---|---|---|---|---|
| FB Oct 15, 2021 (Fri: 52 days) | | | | | | | | | | | | | | | 8 out of 82 Strikes Show 8 \| 18 \| All | | | |
| Trade | Select | ⓘ | 167 | 1,977 | 23.05 | +1.41 | 22.65 | 22.90 | 350.00 | 7.10 | 7.30 | 7.27 | -0.73 | 748 | 3,712 | ⓘ | Select | Trade |
| Trade | Select | ⓘ | 122 | 10,499 | 19.25 | +1.09 | 19.20 | 19.55 | 355.00 | 8.60 | 8.80 | 8.77 | -0.95 | 142 | 8,522 | ⓘ | Select | Trade |
| Trade | Select | ⓘ | 282 | 4,205 | 18.20 | +1.15 | 16.10 | 16.30 | 360.00 | 10.35 | 10.60 | 10.45 | -1.25 | 359 | 1,885 | ⓘ | Select | Trade |
| Trade | Select | ⓘ | 426 | 1,284 | 13.30 | +0.94 | 13.15 | 13.40 | 365.00 | 12.50 | 12.75 | 12.58 | -0.91 | 248 | 433 | ⓘ | Select | Trade |
| Trade | Select | ⓘ | 2,611 | 3,819 | 10.80 | +0.90 | 10.60 | 10.80 | 370.00 | 14.90 | 15.20 | 15.07 | -0.98 | 79 | 962 | ⓘ | Select | Trade |
| Trade | Select | ⓘ | 432 | 3,169 | 8.51 | +0.60 | 8.45 | 8.70 | 375.00 | 17.75 | 18.00 | 17.41 | -1.05 | 13 | 282 | ⓘ | Select | Trade |
| Trade | Select | ⓘ | 1,450 | 4,365 | 6.65 | +0.50 | 6.65 | 6.85 | 380.00 | 20.85 | 21.30 | 21.79 | 0 | 0 | 408 | ⓘ | Select | Trade |
| Trade | Select | ⓘ | 398 | 1,957 | 5.27 | +0.42 | 5.15 | 5.35 | 385.00 | 24.35 | 24.75 | 24.12 | -0.93 | 2 | 113 | ⓘ | Select | Trade |

Source: Charles Schwab

Alice buys 2 contracts of Facebook call options that expire on October 15$^{th}$, 2021. The strike price for the contract is **$350**. Assume that Alice pays the minimum required premium for the stock.

If the Facebook price on October 16$^{th}$ is $400:

    a. How many shares of stock does Alice have the option to buy?
    b. How much premium does Alice pay for the contract? (Assume that Alice pays the minimum amount)
    c. How much profit does Alice make on October 16$^{th}$?

# Call Option 1 (Answers)

📅 **FB Oct 15, 2021 (Fri: 52 days)**

| Trade | Select | ⓘ | 167 | 1,977 | 23.05 | +1.41 | 22.65 | 22.90 | 350.00 |
|---|---|---|---|---|---|---|---|---|---|

Alice buys 2 contracts of Facebook call options that expire on October 15$^{th}$, 2021. The strike price for the contract is $350.

If the Facebook price on October 16$^{th}$ is $400:

    a. How many shares of stock does Alice have the option to buy?
    b. How much premium does Alice pay for the contract? (Assume that Alice pays the minimum amount)
    c. How much profit does Alice make on October 16$^{th}$?


    a. 2*100 = **200 shares**
    b. 22.65*100=**$4530**
    c. Profit = ($400-$350)*200 = **$10000**

Here's the contract for Facebook call options.

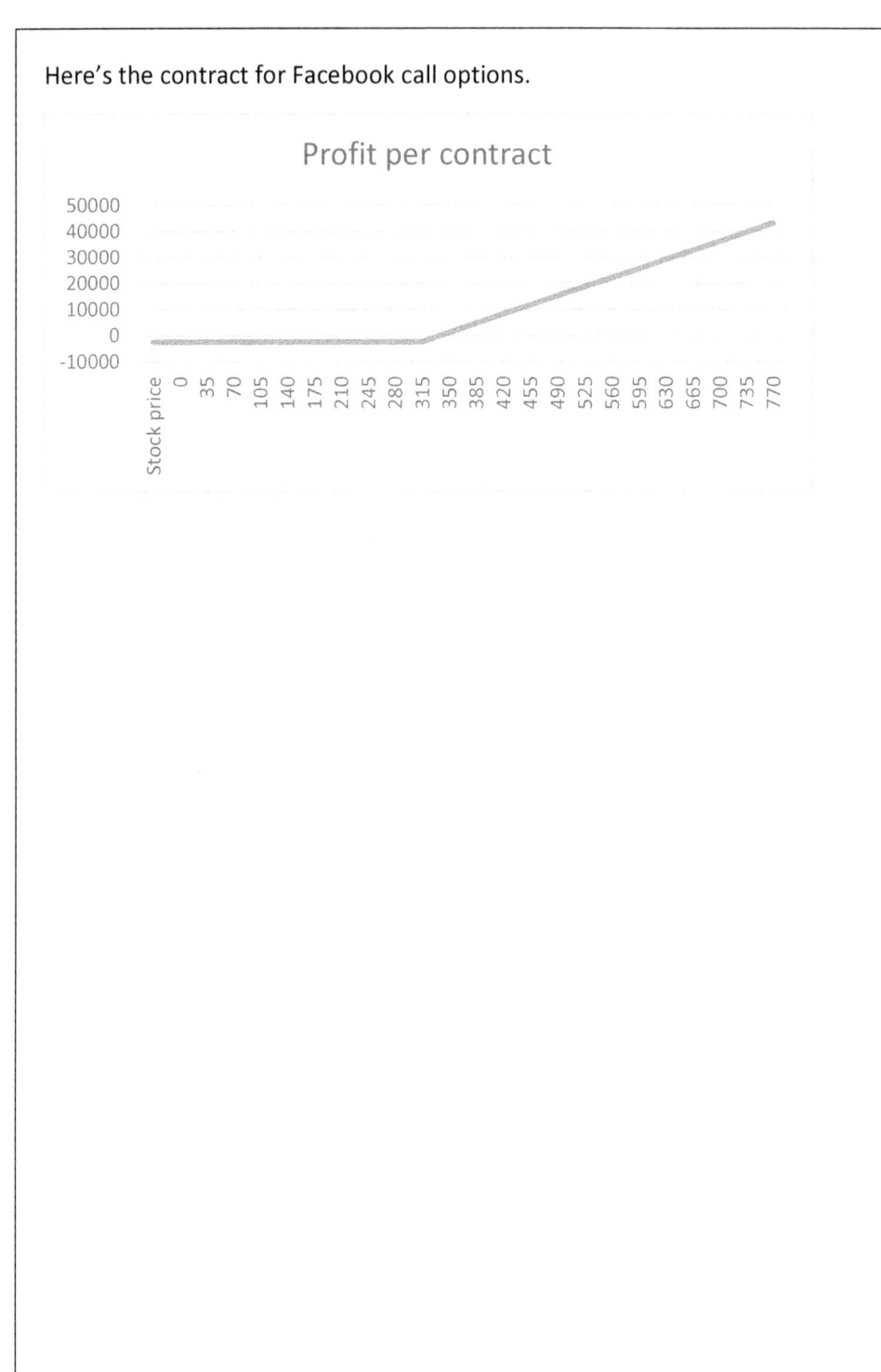

## Call Option 2

| | | | | | | | | | | | | | | | | |
|---|---|---|---|---|---|---|---|---|---|---|---|---|---|---|---|---|
| AAPL Jun 17, 2022 (Fri: 297 days) | | | | | | | | | | | | | 8 out of 79 Strikes Show 8 \| 16 \| All | | | |
| Trade | Select | ⓘ | 59 | 9,845 | 27.10 | -0.05 | 26.95 | 27.05 | 130.00 | 7.20 | 7.35 | 7.35 | 0 | 31 | 10,152 ⓘ | Select | Trade |
| Trade | Select | ⓘ | 8 | 12,081 | 23.60 | -0.15 | 23.45 | 23.65 | 135.00 | 8.80 | 8.90 | 8.65 | 0 | 34 | 9,225 ⓘ | Select | Trade |
| Trade | Select | ⓘ | 161 | 28,302 | 20.40 | -0.27 | 20.35 | 20.50 | 140.00 | 10.65 | 10.75 | 10.70 | -0.04 | 171 | 4,991 ⓘ | Select | Trade |
| Trade | Select | ⓘ | 60 | 13,858 | 17.80 | -0.25 | 17.50 | 17.65 | 145.00 | 12.75 | 12.90 | 12.80 | -0.12 | 174 | 7,900 ⓘ | Select | Trade |
| Trade | Select | ⓘ | 346 | 22,849 | 15.05 | -0.15 | 14.95 | 15.10 | 150.00 | 15.20 | 15.35 | 15.25 | -0.11 | 69 | 4,427 ⓘ | Select | Trade |
| Trade | Select | ⓘ | 85 | 11,398 | 12.77 | -0.32 | 12.70 | 12.85 | 155.00 | 17.95 | 18.10 | 17.70 | -0.31 | 1 | 1,818 ⓘ | Select | Trade |
| Trade | Select | ⓘ | 205 | 21,777 | 10.80 | -0.24 | 10.75 | 10.90 | 160.00 | 21.00 | 21.15 | 20.97 | -0.35 | 13 | 952 ⓘ | Select | Trade |
| Trade | Select | ⓘ | 59 | 9,406 | 9.15 | -0.25 | 9.05 | 9.20 | 165.00 | 24.30 | 24.40 | 24.27 | -1.43 | 2 | 680 ⓘ | Select | Trade |

Source: Charles Schwab

Tim buys 1 contract of Apple call options that expire on June 17$^{th}$, 2022. The strike price for the contract is $150. Assume that Tim pays the minimum required premium for the stock.

If the Apple price on June 17$^{th}$ is $100:

  a. How many shares of stock does Tim have the option to buy?
  b. How much premium does Tim pay for the contract? (Assume that Tim pays the minimum amount)
  c. How much profit does Tim make on June 17$^{th}$?

# Call Option 2 (with Answers)

| Trade | Select | ⓘ | 346 | 22,849 | 15.05 | -0.15 | 14.95 | 15.10 | **150.00** |

Tim buys 1 contract of Apple call options that expire on June 17th, 2022. The strike price for the contract is $150. Assume that Tim pays the minimum required premium for the stock.

If the Apple price on June 17th is $100:

 a. How many shares of stock does Tim have the option to buy?
 b. How much premium does Tim pay for the contract? (Assume that Tim pays the minimum amount)
 c. How much profit does Tim make on June 17th?

 

 a. 100 shares
 b. $14.95*100=$1495
 c. Loss of $1495

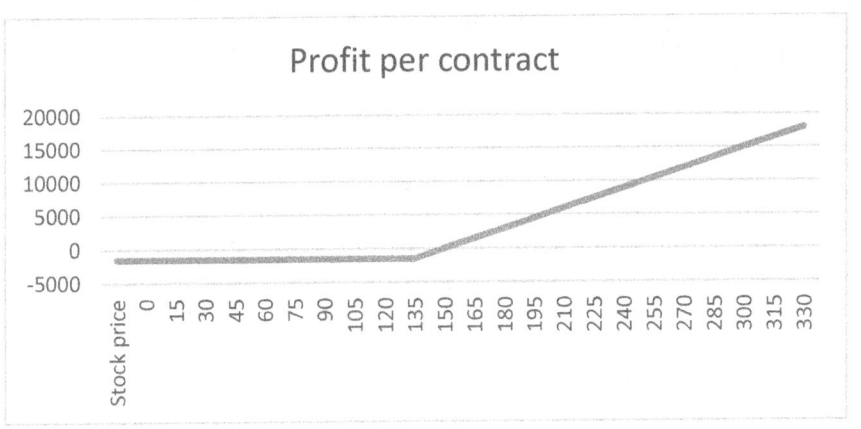

# Call Option 3

| Trade | Select | | | | | | | | | | | | | | | | | | |
|---|---|---|---|---|---|---|---|---|---|---|---|---|---|---|---|---|---|---|---|
| VZ Sep 10, 2021 (Fri: 17 days) | | | | | | | | | | | | | | | | 8 out of 17 Strikes Show 8 16 All | | | |
| Trade | Select | ⓘ | 1 | 0 | 3.20 | 0 | 3.05 | 3.40 | 52.00 | 0.05 | 0.06 | 0.04 | -0.01 | 10 | 48 | ⓘ | Select | Trade |
| Trade | Select | ⓘ | 2 | 6 | 2.20 | -0.46 | 1.93 | 2.23 | 53.00 | 0.09 | 0.10 | 0.09 | +0.01 | 9 | 90 | ⓘ | Select | Trade |
| Trade | Select | ⓘ | 13 | 98 | 1.33 | -0.36 | 1.17 | 1.30 | 54.00 | 0.20 | 0.22 | 0.20 | +0.04 | 1,152 | 3,162 | ⓘ | Select | Trade |
| Trade | Select | ⓘ | 221 | 450 | 0.56 | -0.27 | 0.54 | 0.59 | 55.00 | 0.42 | 0.60 | 0.51 | +0.14 | 1,145 | 4,347 | ⓘ | Select | Trade |
| Trade | Select | ⓘ | 573 | 2,481 | 0.19 | -0.11 | 0.18 | 0.19 | 56.00 | 1.07 | 1.24 | 1.07 | +0.26 | 48 | 1,793 | ⓘ | Select | Trade |
| Trade | Select | ⓘ | 854 | 4,970 | 0.07 | -0.02 | 0.06 | 0.07 | 57.00 | 1.93 | 2.23 | 1.58 | 0 | 0 | 208 | ⓘ | Select | Trade |
| Trade | Select | ⓘ | 8 | 785 | 0.02 | -0.02 | 0.02 | 0.03 | 58.00 | 2.91 | 3.10 | 2.36 | 0 | 0 | 80 | ⓘ | Select | Trade |
| Trade | Select | ⓘ | 0 | 66 | 0.02 | 0 | 0.01 | 0.03 | 59.00 | 3.90 | 4.20 | 0.00 | 0 | 0 | 0 | ⓘ | Select | Trade |

Source: Charles Schwab

Mark buys 5 contracts of Verizon call options that expire on September 10th, 2021. The strike price for the contract is $55. Assume that Mark pays the minimum required premium for the stock.

If the Verizon price on June 17th is $60:

a. How many shares of stock does Mark have the option to buy?
b. How much premium does Mark pay for the contract? (Assume that Mark pays the minimum amount)
c. How much profit does Mark make on June 17th?

# Call Option 3 (with Answers)

Mark buys 5 contracts of Verizon call options that expire on September 10th, 2021. The strike price for the contract is $55. Assume that Mark pays the minimum required premium for the stock.

If the Verizon price on June 17th is $60:

a. How many shares of stock does Mark have the option to buy?
b. How much premium does Mark pay for the contract? (Assume that Mark pays the minimum amount)
c. How much profit does Mark make on June 17th?


a. 5*100 = **500 shares**
b. 0.54*500=**$270**
c. (60-55)*500 - $270 = $2500 - $270 = **$2230**

## Call Option 4

| Trade | Select | | | | | | | | | | | | | | | | | Select | Trade |
|---|---|---|---|---|---|---|---|---|---|---|---|---|---|---|---|---|---|---|---|
| Trade | Select | ⓘ | 50 | 1,835 | 3.36 | +0.33 | 3.25 | 3.35 | 10.00 | 0.21 | 0.22 | 0.21 | -0.05 | 19 | 7,905 | ⓘ | Select | Trade |
| Trade | Select | ⓘ | 88 | 1,971 | 2.54 | +0.29 | 2.45 | 2.50 | 11.00 | 0.36 | 0.39 | 0.37 | -0.08 | 6 | 7,858 | ⓘ | Select | Trade |
| Trade | Select | ⓘ | 160 | 4,824 | 1.77 | +0.25 | 1.73 | 1.77 | 12.00 | 0.63 | 0.65 | 0.67 | -0.09 | 76 | 9,061 | ⓘ | Select | Trade |
| Trade | Select | ⓘ | 1,003 | 12,613 | 1.17 | +0.18 | 1.16 | 1.19 | 13.00 | 1.05 | 1.08 | 1.07 | -0.15 | 62 | 18,812 | ⓘ | Select | Trade |
| Trade | Select | ⓘ | 499 | 18,494 | 0.76 | +0.11 | 0.76 | 0.79 | 14.00 | 1.64 | 1.68 | 1.82 | -0.18 | 84 | 9,018 | ⓘ | Select | Trade |
| Trade | Select | ⓘ | 494 | 21,430 | 0.49 | +0.07 | 0.48 | 0.50 | 15.00 | 2.37 | 2.42 | 2.37 | -0.27 | 66 | 4,085 | ⓘ | Select | Trade |
| Trade | Select | ⓘ | 830 | 15,755 | 0.32 | +0.06 | 0.31 | 0.33 | 16.00 | 3.15 | 3.25 | 3.20 | -0.30 | 403 | 4,122 | ⓘ | Select | Trade |
| Trade | Select | ⓘ | 283 | 6,369 | 0.22 | +0.03 | 0.21 | 0.23 | 17.00 | 4.05 | 4.15 | 4.10 | -0.35 | 20 | 853 | ⓘ | Select | Trade |

F Dec 17, 2021 (Fri: 115 days) — 8 out of 24 Strikes Show: 8 | 16 | All

Source: Charles Schwab

Abhi buys 5 contracts of Ford call options that expire on December 17$^{th}$, 2021. The strike price for the contract is $10. Assume that Abhi pays the minimum required premium for the stock.

If the Ford price on December 17$^{th}$ is $15:

    a. How many shares of stock does Abhi have the option to buy?
    b. How much premium does Abhi pay for the contract? (Assume that Abhi pays the minimum amount)
    c. How much profit does Abhi make on December 17$^{th}$?

# Call Option 4 (with Answers)

**F Dec 17, 2021** (**Fri: 115** days)

| Trade | Select | ⓘ | 50 | 1,835 | 3.36 | +0.33 | 3.25 | 3.35 | 10.00 |

Abhi buys 5 contracts of Ford call options that expire on December 17$^{th}$, 2021. The strike price for the contract is $10. Assume that Abhi pays the minimum required premium for the stock.

If the Ford price on December 17$^{th}$ is $15:

    a. How many shares of stock does Abhi have the option to buy?
    b. How much premium does Abhi pay for the contract? (Assume that Abhi pays the minimum amount)
    c. How much profit does Abhi make on December 17$^{th}$?

    a. 5*100 = **500 shares**
    b. 3.25*500 = **$1625**
    c. (15-10)*500 – 1625 = 2500-1625 = **$875**

# Call Option 5

Source: Charles Schwab

Chen buys 5 contracts of Palantir call options that expire on January 21st, 2022. The strike price for the contract is $25. Assume that Chen pays the minimum required premium for the stock.

If the Palantir price on January 21st, 2022 is $27:

  a. How many shares of stock does Chen have the option to buy?
  b. How much premium does Chen pay for the contract? (Assume that Tim pays the minimum amount)
  c. How much profit does Chen make on December 17th?

# Call Option 5 (with Answers)

| Trade | Select | ⓘ | 1,380 | 47,859 | 3.32 | +0.10 | 3.30 | 3.40 | 25.00 |
|---|---|---|---|---|---|---|---|---|---|

Chen buys 5 contracts of Palantir call options that expire on January 21$^{st}$, 2022. The strike price for the contract is $25. Assume that Chen pays the minimum required premium for the stock.

If the Palantir price on January 21$^{st}$, 2022 is $27:

    a. How many shares of stock does Chen have the option to buy?
    b. How much premium does Chen pay for the contract? (Assume that Tim pays the minimum amount)
    c. How much profit does Chen make on December 17$^{th}$?


    a. 5*100=**500 shares**
    b. $3.3*500=**$1650**
    c. (27-25)*500-1650 = **-$650 (loss of $650)**

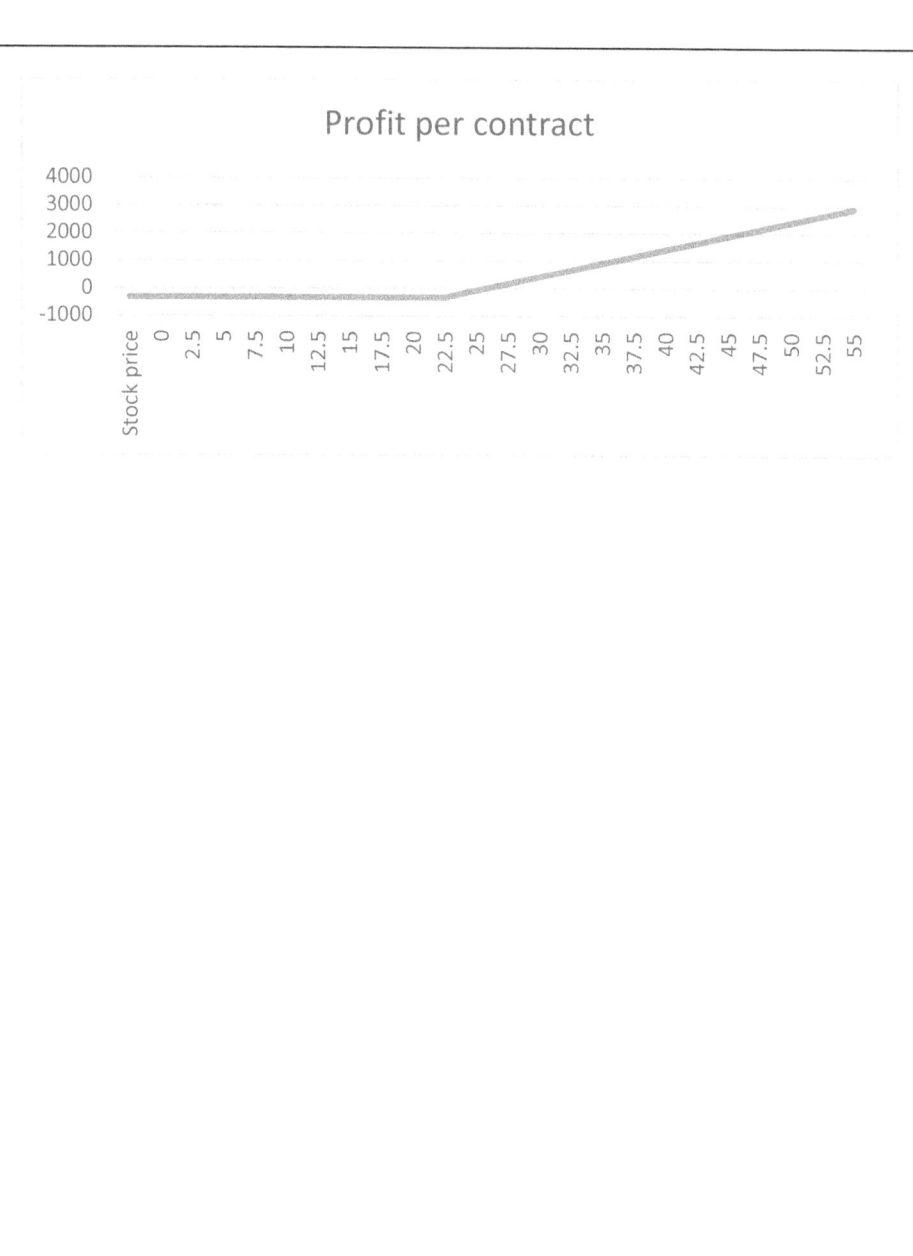

# Call Option vs Buying a Stock 1

| | | | | | | | | | | | | | | | | | |
|---|---|---|---|---|---|---|---|---|---|---|---|---|---|---|---|---|---|
| FB Oct 15, 2021 (Fri: 52 days) | | | | | | | | | | | | | | 8 out of 82 Strikes Show 8 \| 16 \| All | | | |
| Trade | Select | ⓘ | 167 | 1,977 | 23.05 | +1.41 | 22.65 | 22.90 | 350.00 | 7.10 | 7.30 | 7.27 | -0.73 | 746 | 3,712 | ⓘ Select | Trade |
| Trade | Select | ⓘ | 122 | 10,499 | 19.25 | +1.09 | 19.20 | 19.55 | 355.00 | 8.60 | 8.90 | 8.77 | -0.95 | 142 | 8,522 | ⓘ Select | Trade |
| Trade | Select | ⓘ | 282 | 4,205 | 16.20 | +1.16 | 16.10 | 16.30 | 360.00 | 10.35 | 10.60 | 10.45 | -1.26 | 359 | 1,885 | ⓘ Select | Trade |
| Trade | Select | ⓘ | 426 | 1,284 | 13.30 | +0.94 | 13.15 | 13.40 | 365.00 | 12.50 | 12.75 | 12.58 | -0.91 | 248 | 433 | ⓘ Select | Trade |
| Trade | Select | ⓘ | 2,611 | 3,819 | 10.80 | +0.90 | 10.60 | 10.80 | 370.00 | 14.90 | 15.20 | 15.07 | -0.98 | 79 | 962 | ⓘ Select | Trade |
| Trade | Select | ⓘ | 432 | 3,169 | 8.51 | +0.60 | 8.45 | 8.70 | 375.00 | 17.75 | 18.00 | 17.41 | -1.05 | 13 | 282 | ⓘ Select | Trade |
| Trade | Select | ⓘ | 1,450 | 4,365 | 6.65 | +0.50 | 6.65 | 6.85 | 380.00 | 20.85 | 21.30 | 21.79 | 0 | 0 | 408 | ⓘ Select | Trade |
| Trade | Select | ⓘ | 398 | 1,957 | 5.27 | +0.42 | 5.15 | 5.35 | 385.00 | 24.35 | 24.75 | 24.12 | -0.93 | 2 | 113 | ⓘ Select | Trade |

Source: Charles Schwab

Tim is trying to decide between buying investing a $2000 in Facebook call options (Strike price $360) and just buying Facebook stock.

Facebook stock is currently at $350.

Tim pays the lowest amount for the premiums possible.

Calculate the difference in profit after 52 days if:

 i.   Facebook stock is at $400
 ii.  Facebook stock is at $200
 iii. Facebook stock is at $375

# Call Option vs Buying a Stock (Answer)

| Trade | Select | ⓘ | 282 | 4,205 | 16.20 | +1.15 | 16.10 | 16.30 | 360.00 |

Tim is trying to decide between buying investing a $2000 in Facebook call options (Strike price $360) and just buying call options.

Facebook stock is currently at $350.

Tim pays the lowest amount for the premiums possible.

Calculate the difference in profit after 52 days if:

i. Facebook stock is at $400
ii. Facebook stock is at $200
iii. Facebook stock is at $375

Option Premium = $16.1*100 = $1610 per contract

Number of Stocks purchased for $2000 = 2000/350 = 5.7 stocks

|  | Fb Call Option Profit | Buying Fb stock |
|---|---|---|
| Case i | 100*$50 – 1610 = **$3390** | 5.7*(400-350) = **$285** |
| Case ii | -$1610 | 5.7*(200-350) = **-$855** |
| Case iii | 100*$25-1610 = **$890** | 5.7*(375-350) = **$142.5** |

In Case i and iii the call option leads to a higher profit, while Case ii, buying the Fb call option is worse as it leads to a higher loss.

# Call Option vs Buying a Stock 2

**AAPL Jun 17, 2022 (Fri: 297 days)**                                                                 8 out of 79 Strikes  Show 8 | 16 | All

| Trade | Select | ⓘ | 59 | 9,845 | 27.10 | -0.05 | 26.95 | 27.05 | 130.00 | 7.20 | 7.35 | 7.35 | 0 | 31 | 10.152 | ⓘ | Select | Trade |
|---|---|---|---|---|---|---|---|---|---|---|---|---|---|---|---|---|---|---|
| Trade | Select | ⓘ | 8 | 12,081 | 23.60 | -0.15 | 23.45 | 23.65 | 135.00 | 8.80 | 8.90 | 8.85 | 0 | 34 | 9.225 | ⓘ | Select | Trade |
| Trade | Select | ⓘ | 161 | 28,302 | 20.40 | -0.27 | 20.35 | 20.50 | 140.00 | 10.65 | 10.75 | 10.70 | -0.04 | 171 | 4,991 | ⓘ | Select | Trade |
| Trade | Select | ⓘ | 60 | 13,858 | 17.60 | -0.25 | 17.50 | 17.65 | 145.00 | 12.75 | 12.90 | 12.80 | -0.12 | 174 | 7,900 | ⓘ | Select | Trade |
| Trade | Select | ⓘ | 346 | 22,849 | 15.05 | -0.15 | 14.95 | 15.10 | 150.00 | 15.20 | 15.35 | 15.25 | -0.11 | 69 | 4,427 | ⓘ | Select | Trade |
| Trade | Select | ⓘ | 85 | 11,398 | 12.77 | -0.32 | 12.70 | 12.85 | 155.00 | 17.95 | 18.10 | 17.70 | -0.31 | 1 | 1,818 | ⓘ | Select | Trade |
| Trade | Select | ⓘ | 205 | 21,777 | 10.80 | -0.24 | 10.75 | 10.90 | 160.00 | 21.00 | 21.15 | 20.97 | -0.35 | 13 | 952 | ⓘ | Select | Trade |
| Trade | Select | ⓘ | 59 | 9,406 | 9.15 | -0.25 | 9.05 | 9.20 | 165.00 | 24.30 | 24.40 | 24.27 | -1.43 | 2 | 680 | ⓘ | Select | Trade |

Source: Charles Schwab

Sam is trying to decide between buying investing a $15000 in Apple call options (Strike price $150) and just buying Apple stock with that money.

Apple stock is currently at $150.

Sam pays the lowest amount for the premiums possible.

Calculate the difference in profit after 297 days if:

  i. Apple stock is at $100
  ii. Apple stock is at $170
  iii. Apple stock is at $300

# Call Option vs Buying a Stock 2 (Answers)

| Trade | Select | ⓘ | 167 | 1,977 | 23.05 | +1.41 | 22.65 | 22.90 | 350.00 |

Sam is trying to decide between buying investing a $15000 in Apple call options (Strike price $150) and just buying Apple stock.

Apple stock is currently at $150.

Sam pays the lowest amount for the premiums possible.

Calculate the difference in profit after 297 days if:

    i.      Apple stock is at $100
    ii.     Apple stock is at $170
    iii.    Apple stock is at $300

Option Premium = $22.65*100 = $2265 per contract

Number of contracts purchased for $15000 = 6

Number of Stocks purchased for $15000 = 15000/150 = 100 stocks

|          | Apple Call Option Profit        | Buying Apple stock           |
|----------|---------------------------------|------------------------------|
| Case i   | −$2265                          | 100*(100-150) = -$5000       |
| Case ii  | $20*600 − 2265 = **$9735**      | 100*(170-150) = **$2000**    |
| Case iii | $150*600 − 2265 = **$87735**    | 100*(300-150) = **$15000**   |

In all 3 cases, the Apple call option performs better than buying Apple stock

# Selling Calls - Covered Calls for Income

## Psychology behind Selling Calls

Pete has owned Tesla stock for the last 5 years. He bought 100 shares of Tesla stock at a price of $50 per share. The price is now $700 per share.

Pete is happy with his Tesla gains. He, however, is unsure of selling. He doesn't want to sell until it hits $1000 at least.

Pete is also frustrated that Tesla doesn't pay any dividends. He's got to wait until the price hits $1000, which may or may not happen any time soon.

So, what he's done is sell call options at a strike price of $1000.

He gets paid a premium from the buyer of the contract.

If the price hits $1000 any time before the expiration date, Pete has to sell his shares. If it doesn't hit a $1000, Pete just sells another contract and gets paid a premium again.

So, Pete keeps getting paid a premium till Tesla hits a $1000.

This is getting paid to wait for your ideal price. A great extra source of income.

# How Selling Call Options Work – An Example

Let's look at Pete's example.

Source: Charles Schwab

He has 100 shares of Tesla. So, he can sell 1 contract of Tesla call options.

He sells at a strike price of $1000.

So, he gets between $6830 and $7550 for 1 contract of Tesla.

If the stock price reaches a $1000 within 386 days, he must sell his 100 Tesla stocks.

If stock price doesn't reach a $1000 within 386 days, then Pete sells another contract and gets another premium.

## Downsides to Selling Calls

The main downside to selling a call is that the stock price might rise far above the strike price, so you miss out on the upside gain. For example, if Pete's Tesla stocks goes to $2000 per share, Pete missed out on all the gains above $1000, since he sold at $1000.

# Selling Calls Worksheet

All premiums in examples below received are the lowest amount in the range.

## Example 1

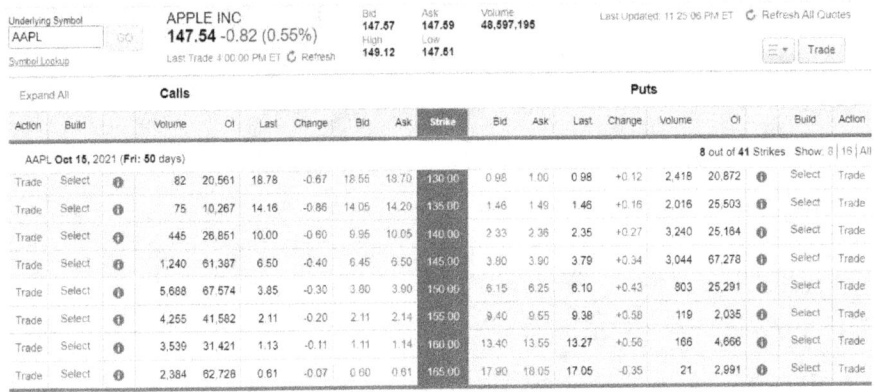

Source: Charles Schwab

Tim owns 250 shares of Apple stock, and he wants to sell call options using information above at a strike price of $165.

    i.    How many contracts can he sell?
    ii.    What is the expiry date of the option?
    iii.    What is the premium that he receives?
    iv.    If after 50 days, Apple is at $200, at what price does he sell Apple stock for?

# Example 1 - Answers

i. How many contracts can he sell? **2 contracts**
ii. What is the expiry date of the option? **October 15th, 2021**
iii. What is the premium that he receives? **$60**
iv. If after 50 days, Apple is at $200, at what price does he sell Apple stock for? **He sells it at the strike price of $165**

# Example 2

Source: Charles Schwab

Jane owns 100 shares of Facebook stock, and he wants to sell call options using information above at a strike price of $370.

    i.      How many contracts can she sell?
    ii.     What is the expiry date of the option?
    iii.    What is the premium that she receives?
    iv.    If after 148 days, Facebook is at $300, at what price does he sell Facebook stock for?

# Example 2 - Answers

| Trade | Select | ⓘ | 50 | 2,724 | 23.89 | -2.06 | 23.75 | 24.00 | 370.00 |
|---|---|---|---|---|---|---|---|---|---|

i. How many contracts can she sell? **1 contract**
ii. What is the expiry date of the option? **January 21, 2022**
iii. What is the premium that she receives? **$2375**
iv. If after 148 days, Facebook is at $300, at what price does she sell Facebook stock for? **Since stock is below strike price, she doesn't sell the stock**

# Example 3

Source: Charles Schwab

Tim owns 570 shares of Palantir stock, and he wants to sell call options using information above at a strike price of $30.

    i.      How many contracts can he sell?
    ii.     What is the expiry date of the option?
    iii.    What is the premium that he receives?
    iv.    If after 295 days, Palantir is at $31, at what price does he sell Facebook stock for?

# Example 3 – Answers

Trade  Select  ⓘ   186   8,818   3.20   +0.30   3.10   3.20   **30.00**

i. How many contracts can he sell? **5 contracts**
ii. What is the expiry date of the option? **June 17th, 2022**
iii. What is the premium that he receives? **$310**
iv. If after 295 days, Palantir is at $31, at what price does he sell Facebook stock for? **He sells at strike price of $30**

# Example 4

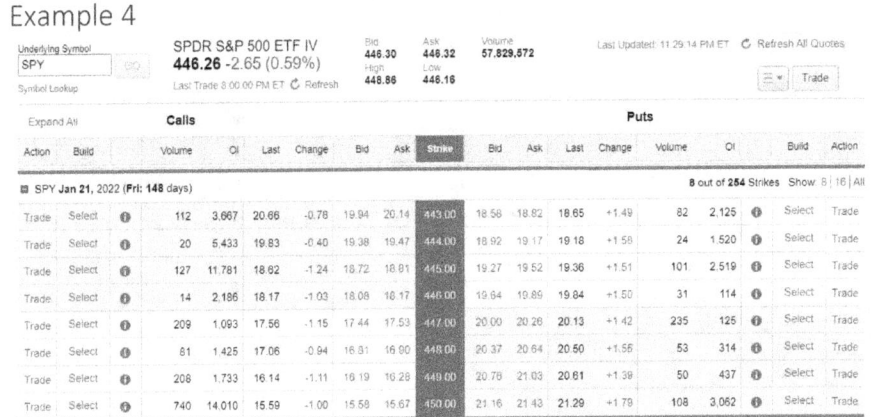

Source: Charles Schwab

Bob owns 50 shares of the SPDR S&P 500, and he wants to sell call options using information above at a strike price of $450.

    i.       How many contracts can he sell?
    ii.      What is the expiry date of the option?
    iii.     What is the premium that he receives?
    iv.     If after 148 days, the stock is at $300, at what price does he sell the stock for?

# Example 4 - Answers

| Trade | Select | ⓘ | 740 | 14,010 | 15.59 | -1.00 | 15.58 | 15.67 | 450.00 |

i. How many contracts can he sell? **He cannot sell any options because he needs a minimum of 100 shares to sell 1 contract.**

# Example 5

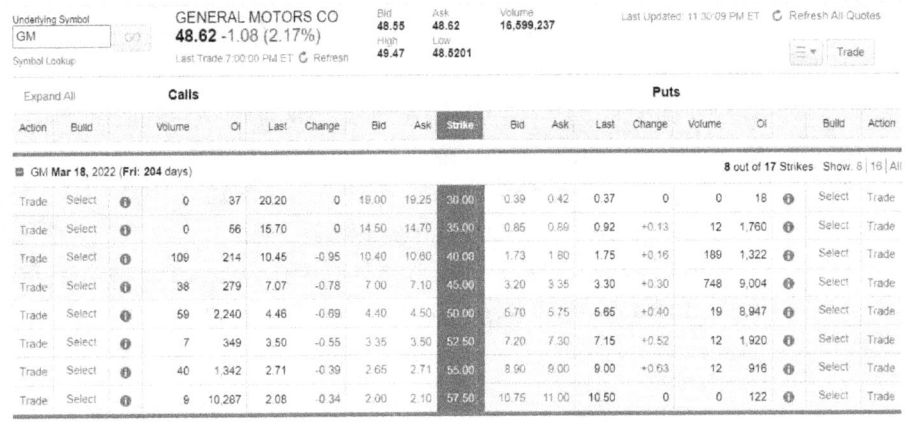

Source: Charles Schwab

Emma owns 300 shares of the General Motors, and he wants to sell call options using information above at a strike price of $50.

    i.      How many contracts can she sell?
    ii.     What is the expiry date of the option?
    iii.    What is the premium that she receives?
    iv.    If after 204 days, General Motors is at $50, at what price does he sell General Motors stock for?

# Example 5 - Answers

Trade  Select  ⓘ   59   2,240   4.46   -0.69   4.40   4.50   **50.00**

i. How many contracts can she sell? **3 contracts**
ii. What is the expiry date of the option? **March 18th, 2022**
iii. What is the premium that she receives? **$440**
iv. If after 204 days, General Motors is at $50, at what price does he sell General Motors stock for? **Sells at the strike price of $50**

# Buying Puts – Protective Put

## Psychology behind a Put Option

Todd Tredsider just graduated from college and got his dream job at Hewlett Packard. He really enjoyed his work and was making a lot of amazing connections at work. One of his friends who worked in the credit department told him that a hot new tech company had bought a lot of HP computers to run their business. The stock had also been listed on the NASDAQ pink sheets.

Using the insider information, Todd spent his entire life savings on buying HP stock. However, in the end the stock crashed and made huge losses.

Now, let's look at the example of Steven Donovan. Steven Donovan interned at Lehmann Brothers and had an emotional attachment to the company. In 2007, he thought that the company was in great shape. That was the only stock in the portfolio.

However, the company went bankrupt, and the stock price went to zero. Donovan's stock portfolio went to zero.

Both Tim and Donovan made a lot of mistakes in their investment. They did not do their research and did not look to diversify. However, the biggest mistake was not protecting against the downside movement of the stock. The only two ways to do that are shorting a stock and buying a put option.

However, shorting a stock is the riskiest investment possible. While shorting a stock, you are borrowing a stock and selling it into the market. You must buy it back from the market later and sell it back to the lender. If the stock does down, you can buy it back at a cheaper price; and sell it to the lender for a profit. If the stock goes up, you must buy it at a more expensive price and make a loss.

The problem with shorting is that the stock can go up an infinite amount, so your losses can be infinite. Shorting can be the fastest way to bankruptcy.

Let's look at the example of example of how Joe Campbell shorted a stock. He's a full-time day trader. He was doing well in his small account, till he started looking into KaloBios, a biotech startup. The company didn't do well, and they announced that they were going to wind up operations soon. When the price of the stock unexpectedly rose, Joe shorted the stock with the strong expectation that it's going to come back down.

Joe was in a two-hour meeting when a company announcement was made that caused KaloBios stock to skyrocket. The stock has exploded high and when Joe came back to his desk, his account showed a negative amount. He was close to bankruptcy on that trade.

Shorting can be the riskiest trade possible and should not be considered an insurance or hedge.

The best way to insurance yourself against a down stock market or the downside movement of a stock is to **purchase a put option**.

Source: Trading Fuel, https://www.tradingfuel.com/top-5-loss-making-stories-in-the-stock-market/

## What is a Put Option?

A Put Option is a contract that allows the buyer of the contract the option to sell 100 shares of a particular stock within a particular time period.

The buyer of the contract may or may not own 100 shares of the stock.

If the buyer owns 100 shares of a stock and buys the put contract, the put contract is a protective put.

If the buyer does not own 100 shares of a stock and buys the put contract, the put contract is a naked put.

We recommend doing a protective put as it ensures that you can exercise the contract.

# How Buying Puts Work – An Example

Let's say you own 100 shares of Palantir Technologies. You bought the shares at $10 per share a few years ago. The stock is now at $24.87. You're happy with your profit, and you're worried that the stock may be overvalued now. You want to lock in your profits and protect against the downside, but you don't want to sell.

Source: Charles Schwab

So, you buy a put option at a strike price of $20.

The put option above is between $2.23 per share and $2.35 per share (or between $223 and $235 per contract). Let's go with $223 for 1 contract.

That means you can sell the stock for $20 anytime in the next 295 days.

So, let's look at what happens after 295 days (at contract expiration). Let's look at three different scenarios.

**Scenario 1: PLTR is at $30 per share.**

You have the option to sell 100 shares of **PLTR** at $20.

You would not sell at $20 because the shares you own are at a much higher price.

So, you would just lose the premium. Think of it like buying insurance that you did not need to use.

Loss = **-$223** (if you choose to hold your PLTR shares)


**Scenario 2: PLTR is at $10 per share.**

You have the option to sell 100 shares of **PLTR** at $20.

So, you would have a gain of $20-$10=**$10 per share.**

So, you gain a profit of $10*100=**$1000**

However, remember that you paid $223 for the premium.

So, Profit = $1000-$223 = **$777**


**Scenario 3: PLTR is at $18 per share.**

You have the option to sell 100 shares of **PLTR** at $20.

So, you would have a gain of $20-$18=**$2 per share.**

So, you gain a profit of $2*100=**$200**

However, remember that you paid $223 for the premium.

So, Profit = $200-$223 = **-$23 (Loss)**


You start making a profit on the premium once the stock goes below **$17.77** and the maximum profit happens when the stock hits 0.

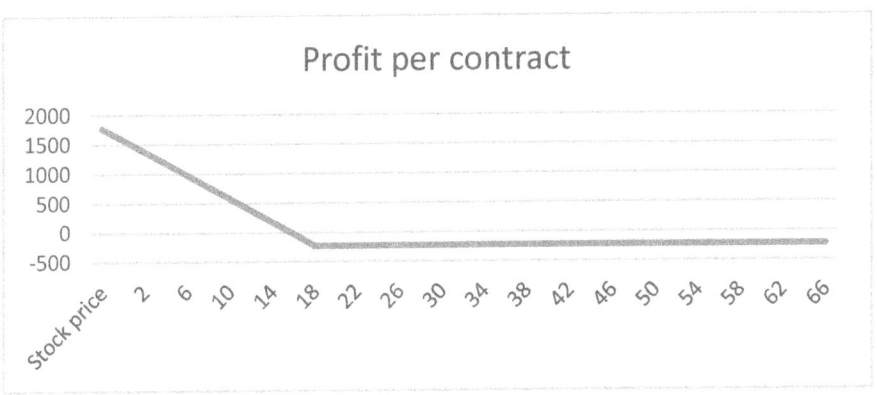

The chart above shows the options graph for Palantir.

If the stock is $20 or above at expiration, the loss is equal to the premium of $223.

The maximum profit for buying a put option is always at $0. In this case the maximum profit is $1777 per contract when the stock hits $0.

So, buying puts is a good hedge against bankruptcy of the company.

## Downsides to Buying Puts

The biggest cost to buying a put is the premium of the put option. You lose the premium each time the stock expires above the strike price.

So, it's like insurance. You keep paying and it may never be utilized.

It's best to buy puts when the premiums are low. The best strategy to figure out when premiums are low is to read the chapter on **Use of Volatility**.

# Buying Put Options Worksheet

## Put Option 1

| Underlying Symbol | | TESLA INC | | | Bid 712.15 | Ask 712.45 | Volume 13,833,783 | | Last Updated 01:50:39 AM ET | | C Refresh All Quotes | |
|---|---|---|---|---|---|---|---|---|---|---|---|---|
| TSLA | | 711.92 +10.76 (1.53%) | | | High 715.00 | Low 702.1001 | | | | | Trade | |
| Symbol Lookup | | Last Trade 4:00:00 PM ET C Refresh | | | | | | | | | | |

| Expand All | | Calls | | | | | | | | Puts | | | | | |
|---|---|---|---|---|---|---|---|---|---|---|---|---|---|---|---|
| Action | Build | Volume | OI | Last | Change | Bid | Ask | **Strike** | Bid | Ask | Last | Change | Volume | OI | Build | Action |

TSLA May 20, 2022 (Fri: 264 days)    8 out of 89 Strikes  Show 8 | 16 | All

| Action | Build | | Volume | OI | Last | Change | Bid | Ask | Strike | Bid | Ask | Last | Change | Volume | OI | | Build | Action |
|---|---|---|---|---|---|---|---|---|---|---|---|---|---|---|---|---|---|---|
| Trade | Select | ⓘ | 0 | 5 | 142.30 | 0 | 133.00 | 148.00 | **680.00** | 102.20 | 115.00 | 103.65 | -1.90 | 1 | 2 | ⓘ | Select | Trade |
| Trade | Select | ⓘ | 0 | 0 | 0.00 | 0 | 128.15 | 143.00 | **690.00** | 107.25 | 120.15 | 112.25 | +2.53 | 8 | 2 | ⓘ | Select | Trade |
| Trade | Select | ⓘ | 0 | 2 | 130.00 | 0 | 124.00 | 138.50 | **700.00** | 112.70 | 125.45 | 117.20 | -0.90 | 19 | 2 | ⓘ | Select | Trade |
| Trade | Select | ⓘ | 0 | 0 | 0.00 | 0 | 119.15 | 134.00 | **710.00** | 118.00 | 131.50 | 125.00 | 0 | 0 | 0 | ⓘ | Select | Trade |
| Trade | Select | ⓘ | 4 | 0 | 122.64 | 0 | 115.00 | 129.10 | **720.00** | 123.10 | 137.00 | 0.00 | 0 | 0 | 0 | ⓘ | Select | Trade |
| Trade | Select | ⓘ | 0 | 1 | 118.68 | 0 | 110.00 | 124.60 | **730.00** | 130.00 | 142.50 | 0.00 | 0 | 0 | 0 | ⓘ | Select | Trade |
| Trade | Select | ⓘ | 0 | 2 | 114.09 | 0 | 106.45 | 119.45 | **740.00** | 136.10 | 147.50 | 140.65 | 0 | 1 | 0 | ⓘ | Select | Trade |
| Trade | Select | ⓘ | 100 | 3 | 110.16 | -0.43 | 103.40 | 115.35 | **750.00** | 140.65 | 154.25 | 147.19 | 0 | 0 | 1 | ⓘ | Select | Trade |

Source: Charles Schwab

a. What is the stock involved in the Options Chain?
b. What is the current price of the stock?
c. What is the expiry date of the option?
d. What is the cost of buying the Tesla put option at $700 strike price? Assume that the cost is the lowest price in the range.
e. What happens if the Tesla stock is above $700 at expiry?

# Put Option 1 (Answers)

| 700.00 | 112.70 | 125.45 | 117.20 | -0.90 | 19 | 2 | ⓘ | Select | Trade |
|--------|--------|--------|--------|-------|----|----|----|--------|-------|

a. What is the stock involved in the Options Chain?
b. What is the current price of the stock?
c. What is the expiry date of the option?
d. What is the cost of buying the Tesla put option at $700 strike price? Assume that the cost is the lowest price in the range.
e. What happens if the Tesla stock is above $700 at expiry?


Answers:

a. Tesla (TSLA)
b. $711.92
c. May 20, 2022
d. $11270 per contract
e. The put option expires worthless as the selling price is lower than current price
   Loss = $11270 per contract

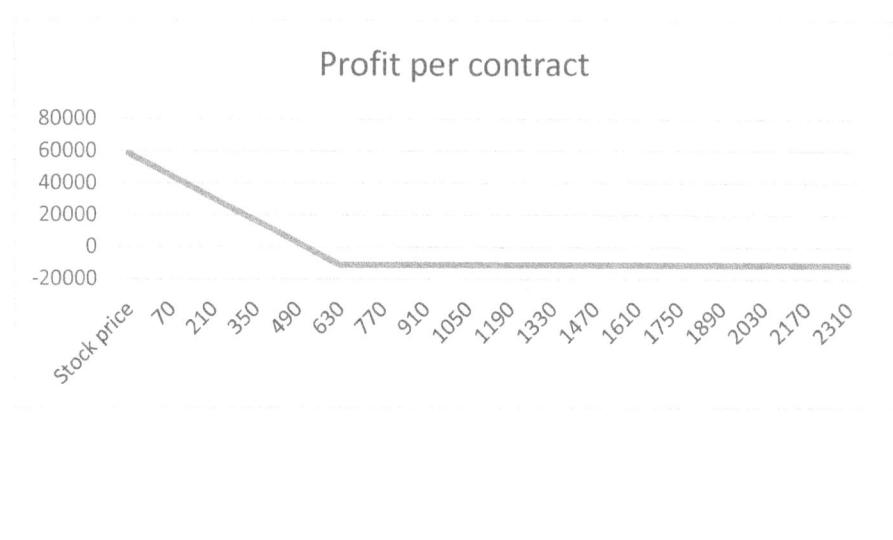

# Put Option 2

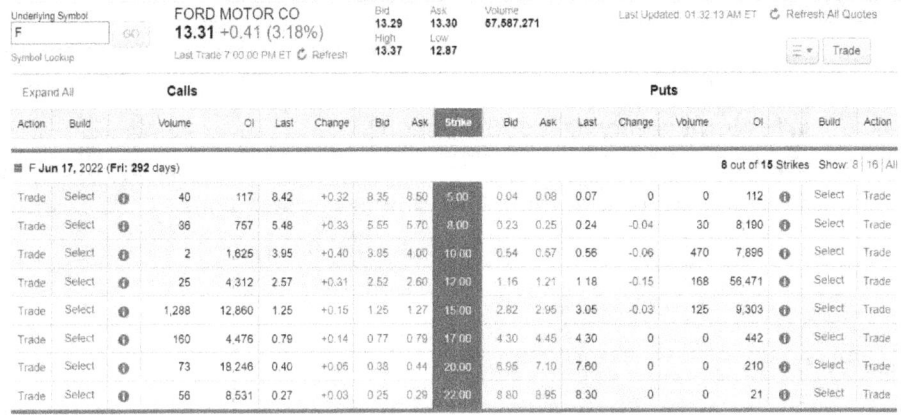

Source: Charles Schwab

a. What is the current price of the stock?
b. What is the expiry date of the option?
c. What is the cost of buying the Ford put option at $12 strike price? Assume that the cost is the lowest price in the range.
d. What happens if the Ford stock is at $5 at expiry?

# Put Option 2 (Answers)

| 12.00 | 1.16 | 1.21 | 1.18 | -0.15 | 168 | 56,471 | ⓘ | Select | Trade |

a. What is the current price of the stock?
b. What is the expiry date of the option?
c. What is the cost of buying the Ford put option at $12 strike price? Assume that the cost is the lowest price in the range.
d. What happens if the Ford stock is at $5 at expiry?

Answers:

a. $13.31
b. June 17, 2022
c. $116 per contract
d. Profit per contract = ($12-$5)*100 – 116 = **$584** per contract

# Put Option 3

Source: Charles Schwab

a. What is the expiry date of the option?
b. What is the cost of buying the General Motors put option at $48 strike price? Assume that the cost is the lowest price in the range.
c. What happens if the General Motors stock is at $35 at expiry?

# Put Option 3 (Answers)

a. What is the expiry date of the option?
b. What is the cost of buying the General Motors put option at $48 strike price? Assume that the cost is the lowest price in the range.
c. What happens if the General Motors stock is at $35 at expiry?


a. January 21, 2022
b. Cost = $330 per contract
c. Profit per contract = ($48-$35)*100 – 330 = $970 per contract

# Put Option 4

Source: Charles Schwab

John buys 3 Apple put option contracts above at a strike price of $145.

- a. How many shares can John potentially sell at expiry?
- b. What is the expiry date of the option?
- c. What is the cost of buying the put option? Assume that the cost is the lowest price in the range.
- d. What happens if the Apple stock is at $150 at expiry?

# Put Option 4 (Answers)

| 145.00 | 15.00 | 15.45 | 15.37 | -0.23 | | 20 | 2.973 | ⓘ | Select | Trade |

John buys 3 Apple put option contracts above at a strike price of $145.

  a. How many shares can John potentially sell at expiry?
  b. What is the expiry date of the option?
  c. What is the cost of buying the put option? Assume that the cost is the lowest price in the range.
  d. What happens if the Apple stock is at $150 at expiry?


  a. 300 shares
  b. September 16, 2022
  c. $1500*3 = $4500
  d. The put option is worthless and John loses the premium

     Loss = $4500

# Put Option 5

Source: Charles Schwab

Steve buys 2 General Electric put option contracts above at a strike price of $100.

    a. How many shares can Steve potentially sell at expiry?
    b. What is the expiry date of the option?
    c. What is the cost of buying the put option? Assume that the cost is the lowest price in the range.
    d. What happens if the General Electric stock is at $50 at expiry?

# Put Option 5 (Answers)

| 100.00 | 4.85 | 4.95 | 4.90 | -1.20 | 36 | 324 | ⓘ | Select | Trade |

a. How many shares can Steve potentially sell at expiry?
b. What is the expiry date of the option?
c. What is the cost of buying the put option? Assume that the cost is the lowest price in the range.
d. What happens if the General Electric stock is at $50 at expiry?


a. 200 shares
b. December 17, 2021
c. $485*2 = **$970**
d. Profit = ($100-$50)*200 - $970 = **$9030**

# Selling Put Options – Selling Cash Secured Puts

## Psychology behind Selling Put Options

Sam has some concerns. He's heavily invested in the stock market in 2007. The market seems to be at an all-time high. He's got a bit of cash in his account; and he's got more coming in from his job.

He's worried about inflation eating away at the value of his cash. But he's also worried about investing in the housing market or stock market, which are both at all-time highs. He doesn't like Gold as it doesn't pay him any dividends. And Gold is at all-time highs at well.

There are very few options available for Sam.

But one of the best available is selling put options.

Sam basically will sell a put options contract, that means he will have to buy a stock if it goes below a certain value within a certain period of time.

Sam gets paid a premium for selling the contract.

So, if Sam notices Apple stock is too expensive at $100; he can sell an option for a strike price of $50 within 3 months. This means that he gets paid a premium and has to buy the stock if it falls below $50 any time in the next three months.

So, Sam gets paid to wait for the stock market to crash.

And the premium he receives is a good inflation hedge; as it gives Sam a return on his cash.

## How Selling Put Options Work – An Example

Let's have a look at Tesla stock TSLA. It's a popular stock that has risen a lot. It's currently around $735.72.

Source: Charles Schwab

You feel that Tesla is overvalued, and you don't want to buy at that price.

You do like the company and would love to buy the company at $250 per share.

So, let's have a look at the put options for Tesla at a strike price of $250

| | | | | Puts | | | | |
|---|---|---|---|---|---|---|---|---|
| Strike | Bid | Ask | Last | Change | Volume | OI | Build | Action |
| | | | | | | 42 out of 42 Strikes Show: 8 \| 16 \| All | | |
| 250.00 | 13.25 | 17.25 | 14.50 | 0 | 0 | 409 | Select | Trade |

The premiums cost between $1325 and $1725 per contract of 100 shares.

So, you get paid $1325-$1725 to sell the contract. This is called the premium for the put option. Let's assume the premium is $1325.

If the put options drops below $250 any time in the next 653 days, you must buy the stock at a price of $250 per share (or $25000 per contract).

So, you need $25000 to buy Tesla stock when that happens.

Some brokerages will ensure that you have the cash between you sell the option. This is called a cash secured put.

Others will let you sell the option without having the cash. This is called a naked put. However, when Tesla drops below $250, you may have to sell other stocks in your account to meet your obligation to buy.

Below is the options chart for selling a Tesla put.

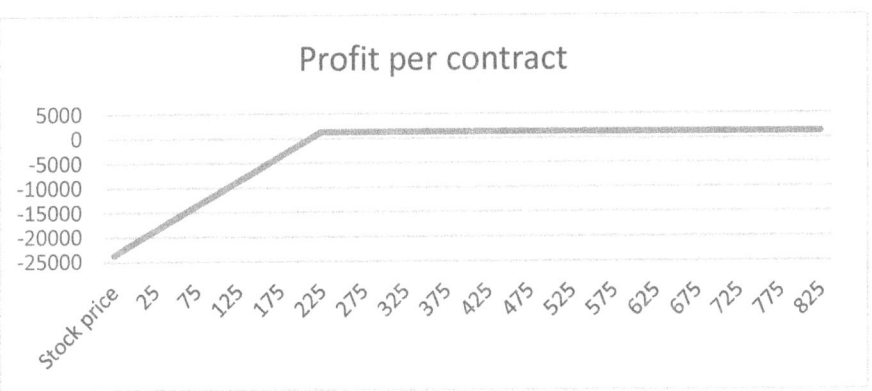

If the stock is above $250 at expiration, you make money on the premium, which is $1325.

The maximum loss happens when the company goes bankrupt and hits $0. In this case, the maximum loss is $23675.

The risk with selling a put option is that the stock might crash much below the strike price.

## Downsides to Selling Puts

The major downside to selling puts is that you need the cash to sell puts. You either need the cash up front for cash-secured puts, or you may need to obtain it later by selling stocks to meet your obligation.

The second downside is you miss out on the upside for the stock. For example, if Tesla rises to $2000, you would have made more money by just buying Tesla stock.

The final downside is the huge loss that happens when the price crashes much below the strike price. Bankruptcy of the company leads to a maximum possible loss, as shown in the example.

Stock selection is key for selling puts. Select high quality stocks with good consistent profits and revenue that have a very low probability of going bankrupt.

# Selling Put Options 1

| | | APPLE INC<br>151.83 +0 (0%)<br>Last Trade 4:00:01 PM ET | | Bid<br>152.47<br>High<br>0.00 | Ask<br>152.50<br>Low<br>0.00 | Volume<br>214,717 | | Last Updated 07:55:42 AM ET | Refresh All Quotes<br>Trade |
|---|---|---|---|---|---|---|---|---|---|

Undedying Symbol: AAPL

| | | Calls | | | | | | | Puts | | | | | |
|---|---|---|---|---|---|---|---|---|---|---|---|---|---|---|
| Action | Build | Volume | OI | Last | Change | Bid | Ask | **Strike** | Bid | Ask | Last | Change | Volume | OI | Build | Action |

AAPL Mar 18, 2022 (Fri: 198 days) — 16 out of 30 Strikes Show 8 | 16 | All

| Action | Build | Volume | OI | Last | Change | Bid | Ask | Strike | Bid | Ask | Last | Change | Volume | OI | Build | Action |
|---|---|---|---|---|---|---|---|---|---|---|---|---|---|---|---|---|
| Trade | Select | 0 | 2,135 | 34.77 | 0 | 34.50 | 34.80 | 120.00 | 2.74 | 2.81 | 2.80 | 0 | 0 | 3,459 | Select | Trade |
| Trade | Select | 0 | 393 | 30.30 | 0 | 30.25 | 30.55 | 125.00 | 3.45 | 3.55 | 3.50 | 0 | 0 | 5,364 | Select | Trade |
| Trade | Select | 0 | 2,248 | 26.25 | 0 | 26.20 | 26.45 | 130.00 | 4.35 | 4.50 | 4.35 | 0 | 0 | 7,115 | Select | Trade |
| Trade | Select | 0 | 2,691 | 22.50 | 0 | 22.40 | 22.65 | 135.00 | 5.55 | 5.70 | 5.70 | 0 | 0 | 7,103 | Select | Trade |
| Trade | Select | 0 | 3,175 | 19.31 | 0 | 18.90 | 19.16 | 140.00 | 7.05 | 7.20 | 7.10 | 0 | 0 | 17,140 | Select | Trade |
| Trade | Select | 0 | 3,439 | 15.89 | 0 | 15.75 | 16.00 | 145.00 | 8.90 | 9.05 | 8.90 | 0 | 0 | 2,827 | Select | Trade |
| Trade | Select | 0 | 10,784 | 13.04 | 0 | 13.00 | 13.20 | 150.00 | 11.10 | 11.30 | 11.20 | 0 | 0 | 5,688 | Select | Trade |
| Trade | Select | 0 | 5,930 | 10.70 | 0 | 10.60 | 10.80 | 155.00 | 13.70 | 13.90 | 13.45 | 0 | 0 | 851 | Select | Trade |
| Trade | Select | 0 | 5,314 | 8.63 | 0 | 8.55 | 8.75 | 160.00 | 16.65 | 16.85 | 16.64 | 0 | 0 | 423 | Select | Trade |
| Trade | Select | 0 | 3,244 | 6.90 | 0 | 6.85 | 7.05 | 165.00 | 19.95 | 20.15 | 19.90 | 0 | 0 | 82 | Select | Trade |
| Trade | Select | 0 | 2,719 | 5.56 | 0 | 5.50 | 5.65 | 170.00 | 23.55 | 23.75 | 26.05 | 0 | 0 | 105 | Select | Trade |
| Trade | Select | 0 | 2,307 | 4.50 | 0 | 4.40 | 4.55 | 175.00 | 27.40 | 27.65 | 27.65 | 0 | 0 | 13 | Select | Trade |
| Trade | Select | 0 | 2,047 | 3.60 | 0 | 3.50 | 3.65 | 180.00 | 31.50 | 31.75 | 32.90 | 0 | 0 | 30 | Select | Trade |
| Trade | Select | 0 | 1,144 | 2.88 | 0 | 2.80 | 2.90 | 185.00 | 35.80 | 36.05 | 41.45 | 0 | 0 | 56 | Select | Trade |
| Trade | Select | 0 | 652 | 2.34 | 0 | 2.25 | 2.33 | 190.00 | 40.20 | 40.50 | 38.95 | 0 | 0 | 16 | Select | Trade |

Source: Charles Schwab

1. When's the expiration date of the options above?
2. What is the premium you would receive for selling 1 put option at a strike price of $120? Assume that you get paid the minimum amount in the range.
3. How much cash do you need as collateral to sell 1 put option at a strike price of $120?
4. What happens if Apple stock is at $130 after 198 days?
5. What happens if Apple stock is at $110 after 198 days?
6. What happens is Apple stock is bankrupt and goes to $0?

# Selling Put Options 1 – Answer

| ASK | volume | | | | | | | |
|---|---|---|---|---|---|---|---|---|
| 152.50 | 214,717 | | Last Updated: 07:55.42 AM ET | | ⟳ Refresh All Quotes | | | |
| Low | | | | | | | | |
| 0.00 | | | | | | | ☰ ▼ | Trade |

### Puts

| Strike | Bid | Ask | Last | Change | Volume | OI | Build | Action |
|---|---|---|---|---|---|---|---|---|
| | | | | | | 16 out of 30 Strikes | Show: 8 \| 16 \| All | |
| 120.00 | 2.74 | 2.81 | 2.80 | 0 | 0 | 3,459 ⓘ | Select | Trade |

1. When's the expiration date of the options above?
2. What is the premium you would receive for selling 1 put option at a strike price of $120? Assume that you get paid the minimum amount in the range.
3. How much cash do you need as collateral to sell 1 put option at a strike price of $120?
4. What happens if Apple stock is at $130 after 198 days?
5. What happens if Apple stock is at $110 after 198 days?
6. What happens is Apple stock is bankrupt and goes to $0?


1. March 18, 2022
2. $274 per contract
3. $120*100 = $12000 per contract. You either need the cash as collateral in your brokerage account, or your brokerage account may make you sell your stocks if needed while executing the contract.
4. The put option expires worthless, and you don't need to buy the stock. The profit is equal to the premium of **$274**.
5. You need to buy the stock at $120. So, you pay $120*100=$12000 for 1 contract. Since the stock is at $110, you are down ($120-$110)*100-274 = **$724 Loss**.

6. Maximum loss of **$11726**

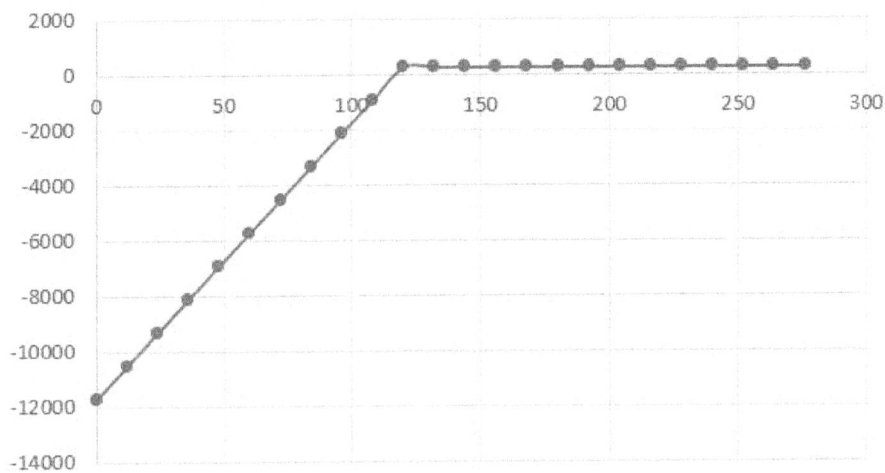

# Selling Put Options 2

| | | | | GENERAL MOTORS CO | | | Bid 49.22 | Ask 49.26 | Volume 8,153 | | | | Last Updated: 07:57:41 AM ET | | C Refresh All Quotes | |
| | GM | | | 49.01 +0 (0%) | | | High 0.00 | Low 0.00 | | | | | | | | |
| Symbol Lookup | | | | Last Trade 7:00:00 PM ET C Refresh | | | | | | | | | | | ≡ ▾ Trade | |

| Expand All | | Calls | | | | | | | | | Puts | | | | | |
| Action | Build | Volume | OI | Last | Change | Bid | Ask | Strike | Bid | Ask | Last | Change | Volume | OI | Build | Action |
| GM Mar 18, 2022 (Fri: 198 days) | | | | | | | | | | | | | | 16 out of 29 Strikes Show 8 \| 16 \| All | | |
| Trade | Select | 0 | 0 | 0.00 | 0 | 8.45 | 8.70 | 43.00 | 2.39 | 2.45 | 2.42 | 0 | 0 | 3 | Select | Trade |
| Trade | Select | 0 | 0 | 0.00 | 0 | 7.75 | 7.95 | 44.00 | 2.66 | 2.89 | 2.73 | 0 | 0 | 202 | Select | Trade |
| Trade | Select | 0 | 281 | 7.43 | 0 | 7.15 | 7.30 | 45.00 | 3.05 | 3.15 | 3.10 | 0 | 0 | 9,754 | Select | Trade |
| Trade | Select | 0 | 3 | 6.75 | 0 | 6.50 | 6.65 | 46.00 | 3.45 | 3.55 | 3.37 | 0 | 0 | 695 | Select | Trade |
| Trade | Select | 0 | 5 | 6.15 | 0 | 5.95 | 6.15 | 47.00 | 3.85 | 3.95 | 3.95 | 0 | 0 | 338 | Select | Trade |
| Trade | Select | 0 | 0 | 0.00 | 0 | 5.40 | 5.55 | 48.00 | 4.30 | 4.40 | 4.40 | 0 | 0 | 331 | Select | Trade |
| Trade | Select | 0 | 30 | 5.15 | 0 | 4.65 | 5.10 | 49.00 | 4.80 | 4.90 | 4.89 | 0 | 0 | 4 | Select | Trade |
| Trade | Select | 0 | 2,242 | 4.55 | 0 | 4.45 | 4.55 | 50.00 | 5.20 | 5.45 | 5.45 | 0 | 0 | 9,709 | Select | Trade |
| Trade | Select | 0 | 333 | 3.55 | 0 | 3.30 | 3.55 | 52.50 | 6.75 | 6.95 | 6.75 | 0 | 0 | 2,179 | Select | Trade |
| Trade | Select | 0 | 1,490 | 2.78 | 0 | 2.50 | 2.68 | 55.00 | 8.40 | 9.15 | 8.50 | 0 | 0 | 950 | Select | Trade |
| Trade | Select | 0 | 10,293 | 2.10 | 0 | 1.97 | 2.04 | 57.50 | 10.30 | 10.45 | 10.45 | 0 | 0 | 127 | Select | Trade |
| Trade | Select | 0 | 2,160 | 1.50 | 0 | 1.48 | 1.54 | 60.00 | 12.30 | 12.45 | 11.95 | 0 | 0 | 659 | Select | Trade |
| Trade | Select | 0 | 361 | 1.20 | 0 | 1.10 | 1.16 | 62.50 | 14.40 | 14.55 | 14.60 | 0 | 0 | 370 | Select | Trade |
| Trade | Select | 0 | 571 | 0.89 | 0 | 0.82 | 1.05 | 65.00 | 16.60 | 17.35 | 16.37 | 0 | 0 | 352 | Select | Trade |
| Trade | Select | 0 | 121 | 0.70 | 0 | 0.61 | 0.82 | 67.50 | 18.90 | 19.80 | 19.25 | 0 | 0 | 128 | Select | Trade |

Source: Charles Schwab

1. When's the expiration date of the options above?
2. What is the premium you would receive for selling 1 put option at a strike price of $43? Assume that you get paid the minimum amount in the range.
3. How much cash do you need as collateral to sell 1 put option at a strike price of $43?
4. What happens if General Motors stock is at $30 after 198 days?
5. What happens if General Motors stock is at $50 after 198 days?
6. What happens is General Motors stock is bankrupt and goes to $0?

# Selling Put Options 2 – Answer

1. When's the expiration date of the options above?
2. What is the premium you would receive for selling 1 put option at a strike price of $43? Assume that you get paid the minimum amount in the range.
3. How much cash do you need as collateral to sell 1 put option at a strike price of $43?
4. What happens if General Motors stock is at $30 after 198 days?
5. What happens if General Motors stock is at $50 after 198 days?
6. What happens is General Motors stock is bankrupt and goes to $0?


1. March 18, 2022
2. $239 per contract
3. $43*100 = $4300 per contract. You either need the cash as collateral in your brokerage account, or your brokerage account may make you sell your stocks if needed while executing the contract.
4. You need to buy the stock at $43. So, you pay $43*100=$4300 for 1 contract. Since the stock is at $30, you are down ($43-$30) *100-239 = **$1061 Loss**.
5. The put option expires worthless, and you don't need to buy the stock. The profit is equal to the premium of **$239**.
6. Maximum loss of **$4061**.

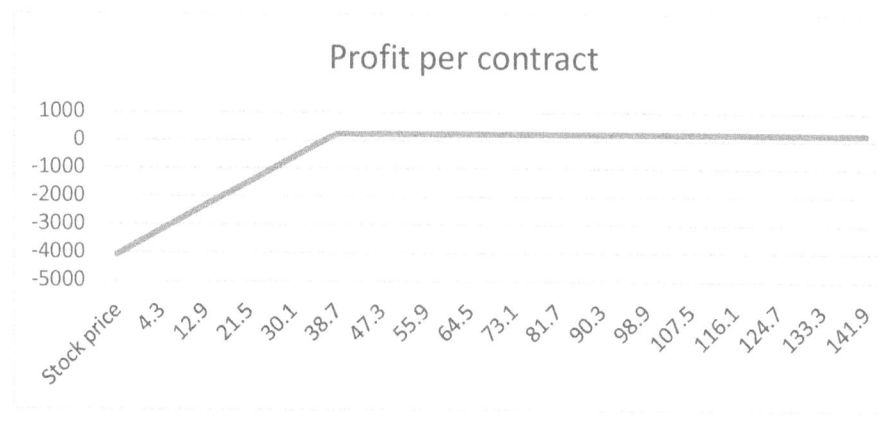

# Selling Put Options 3

| | | | | | | | | | | | | | | | | |
|---|---|---|---|---|---|---|---|---|---|---|---|---|---|---|---|---|
| Underlying Symbol: PTON | | PELOTON INTERACTIVE INC 100.19 +0 (0%) Last Trade 4:00:00 PM ET ⟳ Refresh | | | | Bid 100.30 High 0.00 | Ask 100.45 Low 0.00 | Volume 7,122 | | | Last Updated: 07:58:51 AM ET ⟳ Refresh All Quotes | | | | Trade | |
| Expand All | | **Calls** | | | | | | | | **Puts** | | | | | | |
| Action | Build | Volume | OI | Last | Change | Bid | Ask | Strike | Bid | Ask | Last | Change | Volume | OI | Build | Action |
| PTON Mar 18, 2022 (Fri: 198 days) | | | | | | | | | | | | | | 16 out of 32 Strikes Show 8\|16\|All | | |
| Trade | Select ⓘ | 0 | 195 | 35.70 | 0 | 34.10 | 34.60 | 70.00 | 3.85 | 4.05 | 3.90 | 0 | 0 | 316 ⓘ | Select | Trade |
| Trade | Select ⓘ | 0 | 44 | 45.80 | 0 | 30.15 | 30.90 | 75.00 | 5.15 | 5.35 | 5.00 | 0 | 0 | 1,626 ⓘ | Select | Trade |
| Trade | Select ⓘ | 0 | 41 | 28.95 | 0 | 27.10 | 27.65 | 80.00 | 6.70 | 6.90 | 6.42 | 0 | 0 | 1,218 ⓘ | Select | Trade |
| Trade | Select ⓘ | 0 | 236 | 24.84 | 0 | 23.85 | 24.35 | 85.00 | 8.55 | 8.75 | 8.20 | 0 | 0 | 309 ⓘ | Select | Trade |
| Trade | Select ⓘ | 0 | 68 | 22.75 | 0 | 21.10 | 21.55 | 90.00 | 10.60 | 10.85 | 10.30 | 0 | 0 | 225 ⓘ | Select | Trade |
| Trade | Select ⓘ | 0 | 98 | 19.80 | 0 | 18.45 | 18.95 | 95.00 | 13.05 | 13.30 | 13.00 | 0 | 0 | 124 ⓘ | Select | Trade |
| Trade | Select ⓘ | 0 | 150 | 16.30 | 0 | 16.20 | 16.60 | 100.00 | 15.70 | 16.00 | 15.40 | 0 | 0 | 996 ⓘ | Select | Trade |
| Trade | Select ⓘ | 0 | 339 | 15.25 | 0 | 14.05 | 14.55 | 105.00 | 18.50 | 19.10 | 17.05 | 0 | 0 | 206 ⓘ | Select | Trade |
| Trade | Select ⓘ | 0 | 198 | 13.00 | 0 | 12.15 | 12.60 | 110.00 | 21.70 | 22.05 | 22.19 | 0 | 0 | 806 ⓘ | Select | Trade |
| Trade | Select ⓘ | 0 | 166 | 14.10 | 0 | 10.60 | 11.05 | 115.00 | 25.10 | 25.40 | 17.65 | 0 | 0 | 123 ⓘ | Select | Trade |
| Trade | Select ⓘ | 0 | 126 | 9.40 | 0 | 9.30 | 9.50 | 120.00 | 28.70 | 29.00 | 27.55 | 0 | 0 | 95 ⓘ | Select | Trade |
| Trade | Select ⓘ | 0 | 400 | 8.25 | 0 | 8.05 | 8.25 | 125.00 | 32.40 | 33.05 | 31.55 | 0 | 0 | 736 ⓘ | Select | Trade |
| Trade | Select ⓘ | 0 | 154 | 7.60 | 0 | 7.00 | 7.20 | 130.00 | 36.15 | 36.65 | 33.15 | 0 | 0 | 31 ⓘ | Select | Trade |
| Trade | Select ⓘ | 0 | 613 | 7.10 | 0 | 6.05 | 6.30 | 135.00 | 40.15 | 40.70 | 37.89 | 0 | 0 | 54 ⓘ | Select | Trade |
| Trade | Select ⓘ | 0 | 115 | 6.00 | 0 | 5.25 | 5.40 | 140.00 | 44.60 | 45.00 | 43.05 | 0 | 0 | 26 ⓘ | Select | Trade |

Source: Charles Schwab

1. When's the expiration date of the options above?
2. What is the premium you would receive for selling 1 put option at a strike price of $70? Assume that you get paid the minimum amount in the range.
3. How much cash do you need as collateral to sell 1 put option at a strike price of $70?
4. What happens if Peloton stock is at $50 after 198 days?
5. What happens if Peloton stock is at $90 after 198 days?

# Selling Put Options 3 – Answer

| | Ask<br>100.45<br>Low<br>0.00 | Volume<br>7,122 | Last Updated: 07:59:51 AM ET | ↻ Refresh All Quotes |
|---|---|---|---|---|
| 30 | | | | Trade |

## Puts

| Strike | Bid | Ask | Last | Change | Volume | OI | Build | Action |
|---|---|---|---|---|---|---|---|---|
| | | | | | | 16 out of 32 Strikes | Show: 8 \| 16 \| All | |
| 70.00 | 3.85 | 4.05 | 3.90 | 0 | 0 | 316 ⓘ | Select | Trade |

1. When's the expiration date of the options above?
2. What is the premium you would receive for selling 1 put option at a strike price of $70? Assume that you get paid the minimum amount in the range.
3. How much cash do you need as collateral to sell 1 put option at a strike price of $70?
4. What happens if Peloton stock is at $50 after 198 days?
5. What happens if Peloton stock is at $90 after 198 days?


1. March 18, 2022
2. $385 per contract
3. $70*100 = $7000 per contract. You either need the cash as collateral in your brokerage account, or your brokerage account may make you sell your stocks if needed while executing the contract.
4. You need to buy the stock at $70. So, you pay $70*100=$7000 for 1 contract. Since the stock is at $50, you are down ($70-$50)*100-239 = **$1761 Loss**.
5. The put option expires worthless, and you don't need to buy the stock. The profit is equal to the premium of **$385**.

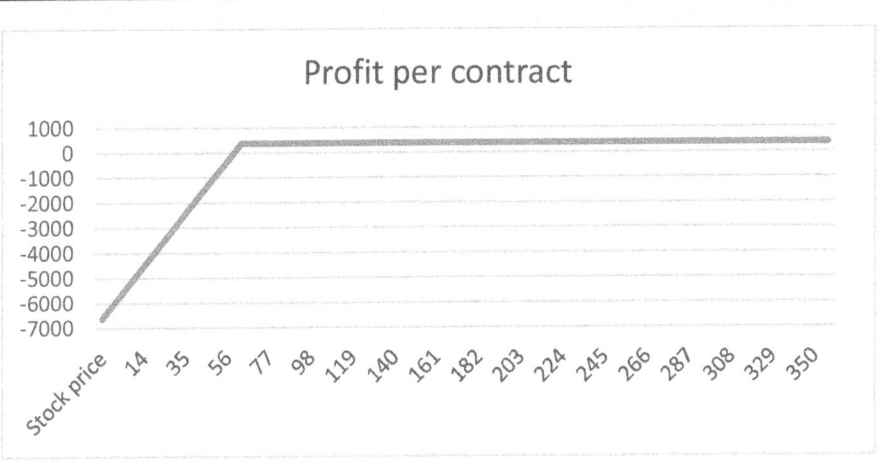

# Selling Put Options 4

Source: Charles Schwab

1. When's the expiration date of the options above?
2. What is the premium you would receive for selling 1 put option at a strike price of $35? Assume that you get paid the minimum amount in the range.
3. How much cash do you need as collateral to sell 1 put option at a strike price of $35?
4. What happens if Verizon stock is at $30 after 198 days?
5. What happens if Verizon stock is at $50 after 198 days?

# Selling Put Options 4 - Answer

| | | | | | | | | |
|---|---|---|---|---|---|---|---|---|
| Ask<br>55.10<br>Low<br>0.00 | Volume<br>8,088 | | Last Updated: 08:01:40 AM ET | | | ↻ Refresh All Quotes | | Trade |

### Puts

| Strike | Bid | Ask | Last | Change | Volume | OI | Build | Action |
|---|---|---|---|---|---|---|---|---|
| | | | | | | 15 out of 15 Strikes | Show: 8 \| 16 \| All | |
| 35.00 | 0.19 | 0.43 | 0.36 | 0 | 0 | 14 ⓘ | Select | Trade |

1. When's the expiration date of the options above?
2. What is the premium you would receive for selling 1 put option at a strike price of $35? Assume that you get paid the minimum amount in the range.
3. How much cash do you need as collateral to sell 1 put option at a strike price of $35?
4. What happens if Verizon stock is at $30 after 198 days?
5. What happens if Verizon stock is at $50 after 198 days?


1. July 15, 2022
2. $19 per contract
3. $35*100 = $3500 per contract. You either need the cash as collateral in your brokerage account, or your brokerage account may make you sell your stocks if needed while executing the contract.
4. You need to buy the stock at $35. So, you pay $35*100=$3500 for 1 contract. Since the stock is at $35, you are down ($35-$30) *100-19 = **$481 Loss**.
5. The put option expires worthless, and you don't need to buy the stock. The profit is equal to the premium of **$19**.

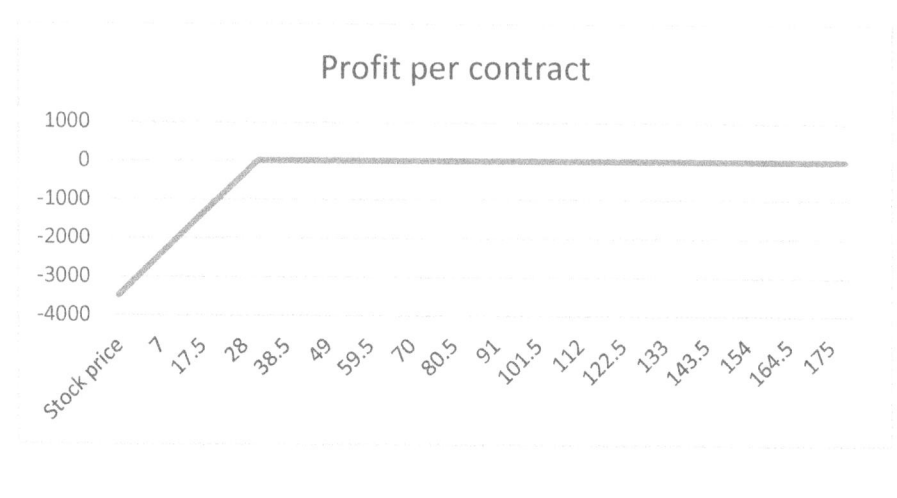

# Selling Put Options 5

Source: Charles Schwab

1. When's the expiration date of the options above?
2. What is the premium you would receive for selling 1 put option at a strike price of $80? Assume that you get paid the minimum amount in the range.
3. How much cash do you need as collateral to sell 1 put option at a strike price of $80?
4. What happens if Taiwan Semiconductor stock is at $78 after 225 days?
5. What happens if Taiwan Semiconductor stock is at $90 after 225 days?

# Selling Put Options 5 – Answer

| Ask 120.11 Low 0.00 | Volume 26,095 | Last Updated: 08:03:19 AM ET | ↻ Refresh All Quotes |
|---|---|---|---|
| | | | ≡ ▾   Trade |

**Puts**

| Strike | Bid | Ask | Last | Change | Volume | OI | Build | Action |
|---|---|---|---|---|---|---|---|---|
| | | | | | | 16 out of 25 Strikes | Show 8 \| 16 \| All | |
| 80.00 | 0.75 | 1.98 | 1.44 | 0 | 0 | 2 ⓘ | Select | Trade |

1. When's the expiration date of the options above?
2. What is the premium you would receive for selling 1 put option at a strike price of $80? Assume that you get paid the minimum amount in the range.
3. How much cash do you need as collateral to sell 1 put option at a strike price of $80?
4. What happens if Taiwan Semiconductor stock is at $78 after 225 days?
5. What happens if Taiwan Semiconductor stock is at $90 after 225 days?


1. April 14, 2022
2. $75 per contract
3. $80*100 = $8000 per contract. You either need the cash as collateral in your brokerage account, or your brokerage account may make you sell your stocks if needed while executing the contract.
4. You need to buy the stock at $80. So, you pay $80*100=$8000 for 1 contract. Since the stock is at $78, you are down ($80-$78) *100-75 = **$125 Loss**.
5. The put option expires worthless, and you don't need to buy the stock. The profit is equal to the premium of **$75**.

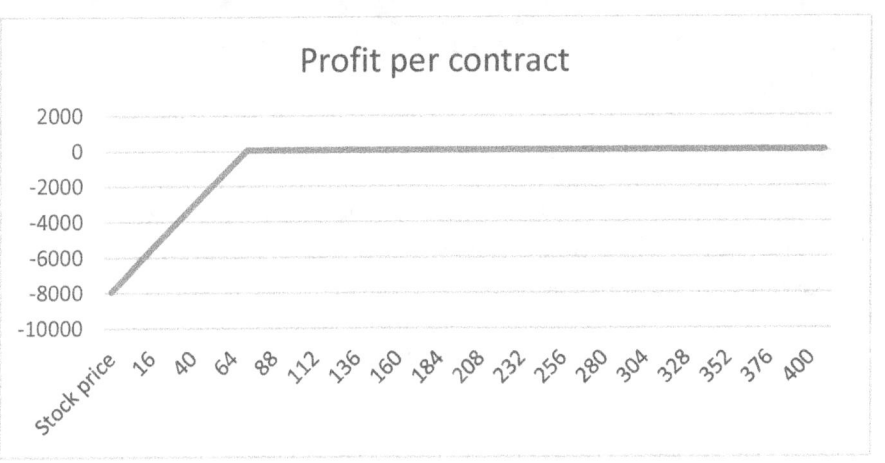

# Intermediate Options Strategies

Welcome to the second part of the book.

Before you start reading this part, make sure that you can buy, sell puts and calls comfortably. Understanding the previous chapters is essential to getting the most out of the rest of this book.

# Spread 1 – Collar

## Psychology behind the Collar

It's 2016. Kabir is heavily invested in stocks. His account has increased a fair amount in the last 3 years. It's been 8 years since the stock market crash of 2008.

Kabir is a little worried that there may be another crash. The financial experts are very worried about the economy and the stock market. The possibility of Donald Trump becoming President was worrying to the financial experts.

Kabir was aware of put options and how they serve as a good hedge against a stock market crash. He buys put option contracts for all his stocks that expire in 2 years. The premiums are expensive, so he spends a lot of money to essentially buy insurance for his stocks.

Two years later, it's 2018. Stocks are up over 30% since Donald Trump go elected. Kabir is happy that his stock portfolio is up. However, his put options have expired worthless. He spent a good amount on put options and is hesitant to buy more.

That's when Kabir heard about the perfect solution. **The collar.**

Now, let's have a look at why a collar is the perfect solution for Kabir.

## What is a collar?

A collar is combination of two options. One first buys a stock (at least 100 shares). He buys a put on the shares to protect against the downside. He then sells a call at a higher strike price on the same shares with the same expiration date. The premium from selling the calls offsets the costs of buying the put.

# How Collars Work – An example

Steve owns 100 shares of Apple. He's looking to insure against the downside on the stock by using a collar.

Source: Charles Schwab

So, he buys 1 put contract at a strike price of $150; and then sells 1 call contract at a strike price of $160.

Assuming minimum premiums are used for both call and put.

At a strike price of $150 above, the put option costs Steven $775 per contract.

At a strike price of $160 above, Steve receives $710 in premium for selling a call.

So, in total Steve pays a total of ($775-$710=) **$65** for the collar.

So, he has the same downside hedge that he would receive if he simply bought a put option. But he pays a fraction of the cost.

So, let's have a look at what happens in 3 different scenarios at the end of expiration:

    a. Apple stock AAPL is at $140
    b. AAPL is at $152
    c. AAPL is at $170

    a. Apple stock AAPL is at $140

At $140, the $140 put option is executed, while the call option is worthless.

So Steve receives ($150-$140)*100 = $1000 from the put option.

But, remember, he spent $60 to buy the collar.

So, his total profit = $1000-$60 = **$940 profit**.

    b. AAPL is at $152

At $152, both call and put options are worthless and cannot be executed.

So, he doesn't gain or lose anything from the option.

So Steve only loses the amount he spent on the collar.

**Loss = $60**

c. AAPL is at $170

At $170, the put option is worthless, and the call option is executed. So, he has to sell his shares at the strike price of $160. He makes money on the increase in share price but loses on the premium

Increase in share price = ($160-$154)*100 = $600

Premium = $60

**Profit = $600-$60 = $540**

However, it is important to keep in mind that he would have made more if he just bought 100 shares at $154 and sold at $170.

So, that's the only disadvantage with a collar. You miss out on the upward movement on the stock.

Keep this in mind while buying a collar.

# Collar 1

Pete owns 200 shares of General Motors. He sells a collar; buying a put at $45 and selling a call at $55. It expires in 133 days.

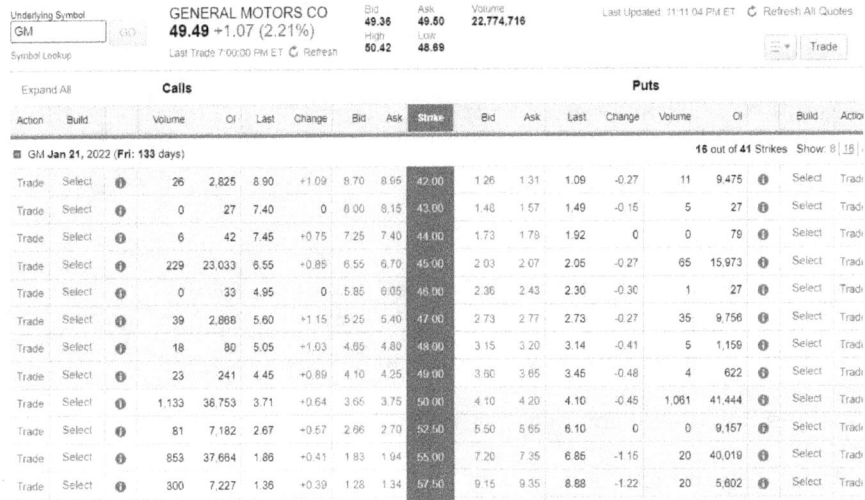

Source: Charles Schwab

a. What is the cost of buying the collar?
b. What happens if General Motors is at $40 at expiration?
c. What happens if General Motors is at $60 at expiration?
d. What happens if General Motors is at $50 at expiration?

Assume that the minimum prices are paid for buying/selling puts/calls

# Collar 1 (Answer)

Pete owns 200 shares of General Motors. He sells a collar; buying a put at $45 and selling a call at $55. It expires in days.

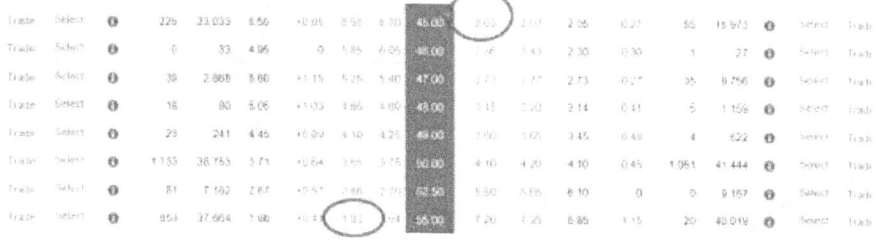

a. What is the cost of buying the collar?
b. What happens if General Motors is at $40 at expiration?
c. What happens if General Motors is at $60 at expiration?
d. What happens if General Motors is at $50 at expiration?

Assume that the minimum prices are paid for buying/selling puts/calls

200 shares = 2 contracts

a. He pays $203*2=$406 to buy the put and receives $183*2=$366 to sell the call. So he pays ($406-$366) **$40** for the collar.
b. The put option expires below strike price of $45, so he gets ($45-$40)*200 = **$1000 profit** for the put option. The call option expires worthless. When subtracting the cost of the collar, he gets $1000-$40 = **$960 profit**.
c. The put option expires worthless. He must sell his stock at a price of $55. The profit/loss for the stock depends on how much he paid for the stock when he bought it. He does lose the $40 for the collar in addition to any loss/profit made from the stock.
d. At $50, both the put option and call option expire worthless. He maintains ownership of the stock, and only **loses $40** for the collar.

# Collar 2

Sam owns 100 shares of Tesla. He sells a collar; buying a put at $700 and selling a call at $760. It expires in 70 days.

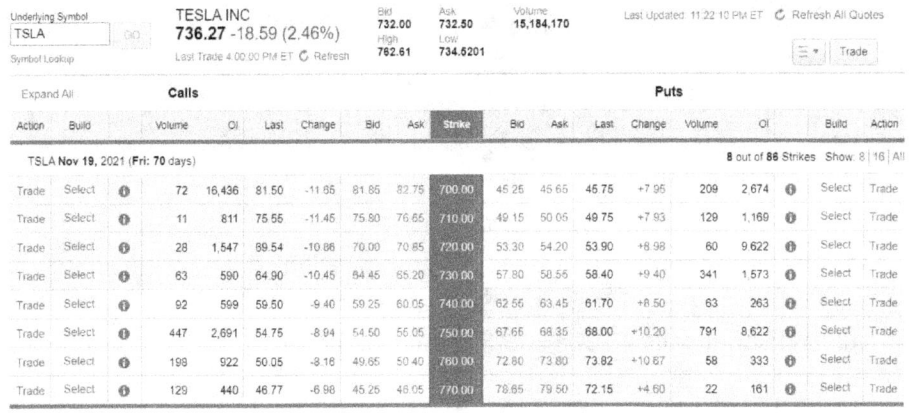

Source: Charles Schwab

a. What is the cost of buying the collar?
b. What happens if Tesla is at $600 at expiration?
c. What happens if Tesla is at $800 at expiration?
d. What happens if Tesla is at $720 at expiration?

Assume that the minimum prices are paid for buying/selling puts/calls

# Collar 2 (Answer)

| 72 | 16,436 | 81.50 | -11.86 | 81.96 | 82.75 | 700.00 | 45.25 | 45.65 | 45.75 | +7.95 | 209 | 2,674 |
|----|--------|-------|--------|-------|-------|--------|-------|-------|-------|-------|-----|-------|
| 11 | 811 | 75.55 | -13.48 | 75.80 | 76.65 | 710.00 | 49.15 | 49.05 | 49.75 | -7.93 | 129 | 1,169 |
| 28 | 1,547 | 89.54 | -10.88 | 70.00 | 70.85 | 720.00 | 53.30 | 54.20 | 53.90 | +8.98 | 60 | 9,622 |
| 63 | 660 | 84.90 | -13.46 | 84.35 | 65.20 | 730.00 | 57.80 | 58.55 | 58.40 | +3.40 | 341 | 1,573 |
| 92 | 699 | 59.60 | -8.40 | 59.25 | 60.05 | 740.00 | 62.55 | 63.45 | 61.70 | +8.50 | 83 | 263 |
| 447 | 2,691 | 54.75 | -3.94 | 54.50 | 55.55 | 750.00 | 67.85 | 68.98 | 68.00 | +10.20 | 791 | 8,622 |
| 108 | 822 | 50.05 | -3.16 | 49.05 | 50.40 | 760.00 | 72.80 | 73.80 | 73.82 | +10.07 | 58 | 333 |

a. What is the cost of buying the collar?
b. What happens if Tesla is at $600 at expiration?
c. What happens if Tesla is at $800 at expiration?
d. What happens if Tesla is at $720 at expiration?


a. Buying a Put = $4525 Paid
Selling a Call = $4965 Received
Cost of Collar = $4525-$4965 = -$440
So, Sam receives $440 for the collar
b. The put option expires below strike price of $700, so he gets ($700-$600)*100 = **$10000 profit** for the put option. The call option expires worthless. When adding what he receives for the collar, he gets $10000+$440 = **$10040 profit**.
c. The put option expires worthless. He has to sell his stock at a price of $760. The profit/loss for the stock depends on how much he paid for the stock when he bought it. He does gain the $440 for the collar in addition to any loss/profit made from the stock.
d. At $720, both the put option and call option expire worthless. He maintains ownership of the stock, and only **gains $440** for the collar.

# Collar 3

Tim owns 100 shares of Microsoft. He sells a collar; buying a put at $290 and selling a call at $310. It expires in 133 days.

Source: Charles Schwab

a. What is the cost of buying the collar?
b. What happens if Microsoft is at $250 at expiration?
c. What happens if Microsoft is at $350 at expiration?
d. What happens if Microsoft is at $300 at expiration?

Assume that the minimum prices are paid for buying/selling puts/calls

# Collar 3 (Answer)

n: 133 days

| 120 | 10.535 | 26.20 | 1.12 | 26.20 | 26.75 | 290.00 | 10.55 | 10.20 | 10.55 | -0.60 | 129 | 6.116 |
| 37 | 4.369 | 22.84 | 1.25 | 22.80 | 23.35 | 295.00 | 12.15 | 12.50 | 12.36 | -0.51 | 158 | 8.523 |
| 68 | 8.828 | 19.80 | -0.93 | 19.05 | 20.15 | 300.00 | 14.00 | 14.35 | 14.31 | -0.31 | 1,422 | 2.706 |
| 77 | 11.890 | 17.00 | 0.62 | 15.80 | 17.20 | 295.00 | 16.20 | 16.50 | 16.25 | -1.00 | 2,387 | 2.845 |
| 1,042 | 16,722 | 14.30 | 0.56 | 14.30 | 14.55 | 300.00 | 18.35 | 18.89 | 18.00 | -0.45 | 1,239 | 4.542 |
| 1,074 | 4.326 | 12.05 | 0.45 | 11.05 | 12.25 | 305.00 | 21.05 | 21.50 | 19.98 | 1.08 | 3 | 650 |
| 173 | 9,012 | 9.91 | -0.48 | 9.80 | - | 310.00 | 24.00 | 24.45 | 21.83 | 1.12 | 0 | 691 |

a. What is the cost of buying the collar?
b. What happens if Microsoft is at $250 at expiration?
c. What happens if Microsoft is at $350 at expiration?
d. What happens if Microsoft is at $300 at expiration?

a. Buying a Put = $1400 Paid
Selling a Call = $980 Received
Cost of Collar = $1400-$980 = $420
So, Tim paid **$420 for the collar**
b. The put option expires below strike price of $290, so he gets ($290-$250)*100 = **$4000 profit** for the put option. The call option expires worthless. When subtracting what he paid for the collar, he gets $4000-$420 = **$3580 profit**.
c. The put option expires worthless. He has to sell his stock at a price of $310. The profit/loss for the stock depends on how much he paid for the stock when he bought it. He does lose the $420 for the collar in addition to any loss/profit made from the stock.
d. At $300, both the put option and call option expire worthless. He maintains ownership of the stock, and only **loses $420** for the collar.

# Collar 4

Abhi owns 500 shares of NAT stock. He sells a collar; buying a put at $2 and selling a call at $3. It expires in 133 days.

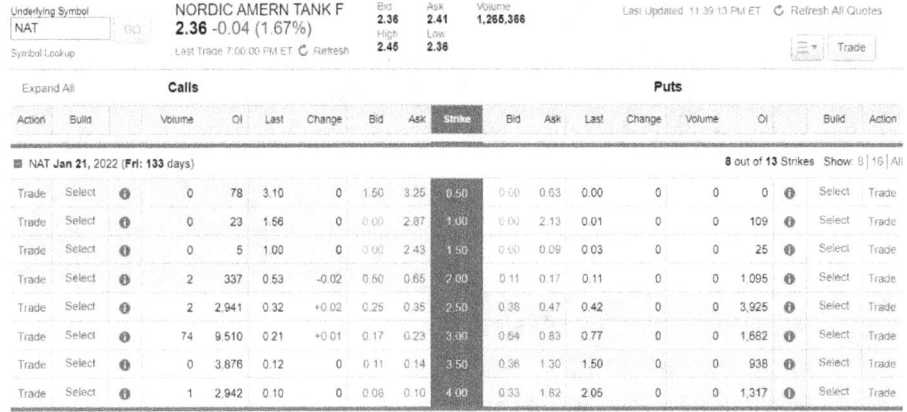

Source: Charles Schwab

a. What is the cost of buying the collar?
b. What happens if NAT is at $1.5 at expiration?
c. What happens if NAT is at $3.5 at expiration?
d. What happens if NAT is at $2.5 at expiration?

Assume that the minimum prices are paid for buying/selling puts/calls

# Collar 4 (Answer)

| | | | | | | | | | | | | |
|---|---|---|---|---|---|---|---|---|---|---|---|---|
| 2 | 337 | 0.53 | 0.02 | 0.60 | 0.85 | 2.00 | 0.51 | 0.17 | 0.11 | 0 | 0 | 1.095 |
| 2 | 2.941 | 0.32 | -0.02 | 0.25 | 1.06 | 2.50 | 0.38 | 0.47 | 0.42 | 0 | 0 | 3.925 |
| 74 | 0.510 | 0.21 | -0.03 | 0.12 | 0.23 | 3.00 | 0.64 | 0.85 | 0.77 | 0 | 0 | 1.682 |

a. What is the cost of buying the collar?
b. What happens if NAT is at $1.5 at expiration?
c. What happens if NAT is at $3.5 at expiration?
d. What happens if NAT is at $2.5 at expiration?

500 shares = 5 contracts
a. Buying a Put = $11*5=$55 Paid
   Selling a Call = $17*5=$85 Received
   Cost of Collar = $55-$85 = -$30
   So, Abhi receives **$30 for the collar**
b. The put option expires below strike price of $2, so he gets ($1.5-$2)*500 = **$250 profit** for the put option. The call option expires worthless. When adding what he receives for the collar, he gets $250+$30 = **$280 profit**.
c. The put option expires worthless. He has to sell his stock at a price of $3. The profit/loss for the stock depends on how much he paid for the stock when he bought it. He does gain the $20 for the collar in addition to any loss/profit made from the stock.
d. At $3.5, both the put option and call option expire worthless. He maintains ownership of the stock, and only **gains $30** for the collar.

## Collar 5

Bobby owns 100 shares of Schwab stock SCHB. He sells a collar; buying a put at $105 and selling a call at $108. It expires in 133 days.

Source: Charles Schwab

a. What is the cost of buying the collar?
b. What happens if Schwab is at $80 at expiration?
c. What happens if NAT is at $130 at expiration?
d. What happens if NAT is at $115 at expiration?

Assume that the minimum prices are paid for buying/selling puts/calls

# Collar 5 (Answer)

| Underlying Symbol | SCHWAB U.S. BROAD MAR... | Bid | Ask | Volume | | | |
|---|---|---|---|---|---|---|---|
| SCHB | 107.66 -0.85 (0.78%) | 107.11 | 108.89 | 421,789 | | | |
| | | 109.12 | 107.5959 | | | | Trade |

| | Calls | | | | | | | Puts | | | | |
|---|---|---|---|---|---|---|---|---|---|---|---|---|
| Action | Build | Volume | OI | Last | Change | Bid | Ask | Strike | Bid | Ask | Last | Change | Volume | OI | Build | Action |

**SCHB Jan 21, 2022 (Fri) 133 days** — 8 out of 39 Strikes, Show

| Trade | Select | | 0 | 3 | 4.95 | 0 | 6.10 | 1.10 | 104.00 | 2.04 | 2.10 | 0.00 | 0 | 0 | 1 | Select | Trade |
| Trade | Select | | 0 | 9 | 5.28 | 0 | 5.40 | 0.45 | 105.00 | 1.25 | 1.11 | 4.82 | 0 | 0 | 13 | Select | Trade |
| Trade | Select | | 1 | 9 | 5.31 | +0.01 | 4.20 | 8.80 | 106.00 | 1.40 | 4.35 | 0.00 | 0 | 0 | 2 | Select | Trade |
| Trade | Select | | 0 | 0 | 0.00 | 0 | 4.10 | 5.20 | 107.00 | 3.90 | 5.10 | 0.00 | 0 | 0 | 0 | Select | Trade |
| Trade | Select | | 0 | 4 | 3.83 | 0 | 1.40 | 4.10 | 108.00 | 4.00 | 5.20 | 0.00 | 0 | 0 | 0 | Select | Trade |
| Trade | Select | | 0 | 37 | 4.83 | 0 | 2.50 | 1.30 | 109.00 | 4.70 | 5.70 | 0.00 | 0 | 0 | 0 | Select | Trade |
| Trade | Select | | 0 | 1 | 3.26 | 0 | 1.25 | 0.45 | 110.00 | 5.25 | 5.80 | 0.00 | 0 | 0 | 0 | Select | Trade |
| Trade | Select | | 0 | 9 | 2.65 | 0 | 1.00 | 2.25 | 111.00 | 5.40 | 6.50 | 0.00 | 0 | 0 | 0 | Select | Trade |

a. What is the cost of buying the collar?
b. What happens if Schwab is at $80 at expiration?
c. What happens if NAT is at $130 at expiration?
d. What happens if NAT is at $108 at expiration?

a. Buying a Put = $320=$320 Paid
   Selling a Call = $125=$125 Received
   Cost of Collar = $320-$125 = $195
   So, Bobby pays **$195 for the collar**
b. The put option expires below strike price of $100, so he gets ($105-$80)*100 = **$2500 profit** for the put option. The call option expires worthless. When adding what he receives for the collar, he gets $2500-$195 = **$2305 profit**.
c. The put option expires worthless. He has to sell his stock at a price of $115. The profit/loss for the stock depends on how much he paid for the stock when he bought it. He does lose the $195 for the collar in addition to any loss/profit made from the stock.
d. At $108, both the put option and call option expire worthless. He maintains ownership of the stock, and only **loses $195** for the collar.

# Spread 2 – Vertical Bear Call Spread

## Psychology Behind the Vertical Call Spread

As we learnt earlier (from the Selling Calls chapter), Pete made a lot of money selling calls on Tesla. He sold Tesla calls at a strike price of $1000 and received a premium of about $7000 for 1 contract.

However, let's have a look at what happened.

At expiration of the contract, Tesla shot up to $2000 per share. Pete had to sell all his shares at $1000 per share. He still made a profit on his sale of Tesla since he bought at a much lower price of $50 per share. He also received a high premium of $7000 for selling the call option contract.

However, Pete did miss out on the explosion of the stock to $2000 per share.

There is a way where Pete could have received the benefit of the premium while not missing out on the upside of Tesla stock.

Timmy is in a similar position to Pete. He owns 100 shares of Tesla stock. Timmy sells the same options contract as Pete at a strike price of $1000 per share.

However, Timmy also buys a call option at a slightly higher strike price of $1100 per share. So, the premium he receives is a little lower as he must spend some of it buying the call. In exchange, Timmy gets to gain from the upper movement of the stock past $1100. This is a vertical bear call spread.

## What is a Vertical Bear Call Spread?

A vertical call spread consists of buying a call and selling a call at the same expiration date but with different strike prices. Selling a call is done at a lower strike price with a higher premium. Buying a call is done at a higher strike price so it has a lower premium.

The premium received by selling the call is higher than the premium used for buying the call. So, there is a net positive premium.

# How Vertical Call Spreads Work – An Example

Let's have a look at Timmy's example.

Source: Charles Schwab

He has 100 shares of Tesla. So, he can sell 1 contract of Tesla call options.

He sells at a strike price of $1000. Let's assume that he gets the minimum premium in the range.

So, he gets between $6830 for 1 contract of Tesla.

If the stock price reaches a $1000 within 386 days, he must sell his 100 Tesla stocks.

If stock price doesn't reach a $1000 within 386 days, then Timmy sells another contract and gets another premium.

Now, Timmy also buys a call option at a strike price of $1100.

| Trade | Select | ⓘ | 228 | 5,042 | 46.80 | -9.15 | 46.70 | 51.50 | 1,100.00 |

He pays $4670 for the call option.

So, his net premium decreases. He gets a net premium of ($6830-$4670) **$2160**.

So, if Tesla is above $1100 at expiration; Timmy has the option to buy Tesla at $1100.

So, let's have a look at a few different scenarios:

a. Tesla is at $800 at expiration
b. Tesla is at $1050 at expiration
c. Tesla is at $2000 at expiration

**Scenario a:**

If Tesla is at $800 per share at expiration, then Timmy keeps his Tesla shares. And nothing else happens. He just keeps his **net premium of $2160** on the options contract.

**Scenario b:**

If Tesla is at $1050, Timmy must sell his 100 Tesla shares for $1000 per share. So, he loses ($1050-$1000)*100 = $5000 total loss.

His call option expires worthless as the stock is less than $1100 per share.

Since, he received $2160 premium,

His net loss = $5000-$2160 = **$3840 Loss**

This does not take into account any profit or loss he made on selling the shares (which depends on the cost price of the shares).

## Scenario c:

If Tesla is $2000 per share, Timmy has to sell his shares at $1000 per share. However, he has the option to buy 100 shares at $1100 and sell it at a profit of $900 per share.

Timmy's loss on selling the call at $1000 = $(2000-1000)*100 = $100000

Timmy's profit on buying call at $1100 = ($2000-$1100)*100 = $90000

Timmy also received a premium of $2160.

Timmy's total loss = $90000 + $2160 - $100000 = **$7840 loss**

Timmy makes a net loss of $7840 for any amount above $1100 Tesla share price at expiration.

This does not take into account any profit or loss he made on selling the shares (which depends on the cost price of the shares).

Below chart shows a graph of the profit that Timmy makes on the contract versus stock price at expiration.

# Vertical Bear Call Spreads Worksheet

## Vertical Call Spread Option 1

| | | | | | | Calls | | | | | | | | Puts | | | | | |
|---|---|---|---|---|---|---|---|---|---|---|---|---|---|---|---|---|---|---|---|
| Action | Build | | Volume | OI | Last | Change | Bid | Ask | Strike | Bid | Ask | Last | Change | Volume | OI | | Build | Action |
| | AAPL Oct 15, 2021 (Fri: 50 days) | | | | | | | | | | | | | | | 8 out of 41 Strikes Show 8 \| 16 \| All | | |
| Trade | Select | | 82 | 20,561 | 18.78 | -0.67 | 18.55 | 18.70 | 130.00 | 0.98 | 1.00 | 0.98 | +0.12 | 2,418 | 20,872 | | Select | Trade |
| Trade | Select | | 75 | 10,267 | 14.16 | -0.86 | 14.05 | 14.20 | 135.00 | 1.46 | 1.49 | 1.46 | +0.16 | 2,016 | 25,503 | | Select | Trade |
| Trade | Select | | 445 | 26,851 | 10.00 | -0.60 | 9.95 | 10.05 | 140.00 | 2.33 | 2.36 | 2.35 | +0.27 | 3,240 | 25,164 | | Select | Trade |
| Trade | Select | | 1,240 | 61,387 | 6.50 | -0.40 | 6.45 | 6.50 | 145.00 | 3.80 | 3.90 | 3.79 | +0.34 | 3,044 | 67,278 | | Select | Trade |
| Trade | Select | | 5,688 | 67,574 | 3.85 | -0.30 | 3.80 | 3.90 | 150.00 | 6.15 | 6.25 | 6.10 | +0.43 | 803 | 25,291 | | Select | Trade |
| Trade | Select | | 4,255 | 41,582 | 2.11 | -0.20 | 2.11 | 2.14 | 155.00 | 9.40 | 9.55 | 9.38 | +0.58 | 119 | 2,035 | | Select | Trade |
| Trade | Select | | 3,539 | 31,421 | 1.13 | -0.11 | 1.11 | 1.14 | 160.00 | 13.40 | 13.55 | 13.27 | +0.56 | 166 | 4,666 | | Select | Trade |
| Trade | Select | | 2,384 | 62,728 | 0.61 | -0.07 | 0.60 | 0.61 | 165.00 | 17.90 | 18.05 | 17.05 | -0.35 | 21 | 2,991 | | Select | Trade |

Source: Charles Schwab

Tim owns 250 shares of Apple stock, and he wants to complete a vertical spread where he sells a call option at $160 and buy a call option at $165.

   i.  How many contracts can he sell?
   ii. What is the net premium that he receives?
   iii. What happens if Apple stock is at $140 at expiration?
   iv. What happens if Apple stock is at $170 at expiration?

# Vertical Call Spread Option 1 (Answers)

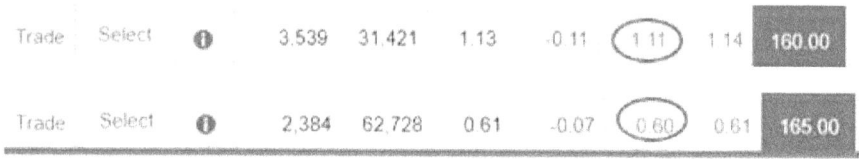

| Trade | Select | | 3,539 | 31,421 | 1.13 | -0.11 | 1.11 | 1.14 | 160.00 |
| Trade | Select | | 2,384 | 62,728 | 0.61 | -0.07 | 0.60 | 0.61 | 165.00 |

i. How many contracts can he sell?
ii. What is the net premium that he receives?
iii. What happens if Apple stock is at $140 at expiration?
iv. What happens if Apple stock is at $170 at expiration?


i. **2 contracts**
ii. Net Premium = 2*111 – 2*60 = **$102 premium**
iii. Both calls expire worthless. Tim keeps ownership of the stocks and his profit is the premium of $102.
iv. Tim has to sell his shares at $165. So he loses ($170-$165)*2*100 = $1000 on the option. He still receives $102 premium. So he has a **net loss of $898** ($1000 - $102). This does not take into account any profits or losses made on the actual sales, which depends on the buying price.

Here's the contract for Apple vertical spread.

# Vertical Call Spread Option 2

Source: Charles Schwab

Jane owns 100 shares of Facebook stock, and she wants to complete a vertical spread where she sells a call option at $370 and buys a call option at $380.

    i.    What is the net premium that she receives?
    ii.    What happens if Facebook stock is at $375 at expiration?
    iii.    What happens if Facebook stock is at $400 at expiration?

# Vertical Call Spread Option 2 (with Answers)

| Trade | Select | ⓘ | 50 | 2,724 | 23.89 | -2.06 | (23.75) | 24.00 | 370.00 |
|-------|--------|---|----|-------|-------|-------|---------|-------|--------|
| Trade | Select | ⓘ | 39 | 4,913 | 19.28 | -1.87 | (19.20) | 19.45 | 380.00 |

i. What is the net premium that she receives?
ii. What happens if Facebook stock is at $375 at expiration?
iii. What happens if Facebook stock is at $400 at expiration?

i. $2375-$1920 = **$455 Premium**
ii. The $380 call option expires worthless. She loses on the $370 call option. She loses ($375-$370)*100 = $500
Since she gains a premium of $455, **her net loss = $45** ($500-$455)
iii. She loses on the $370 call = ($400-$370)*100 = $3000
She gains on the $380 call = ($400-$380)*100 = $2000
If you add the $455 profit, we get
Total Loss = $3000 - $2000 - $455 = **$545 loss**

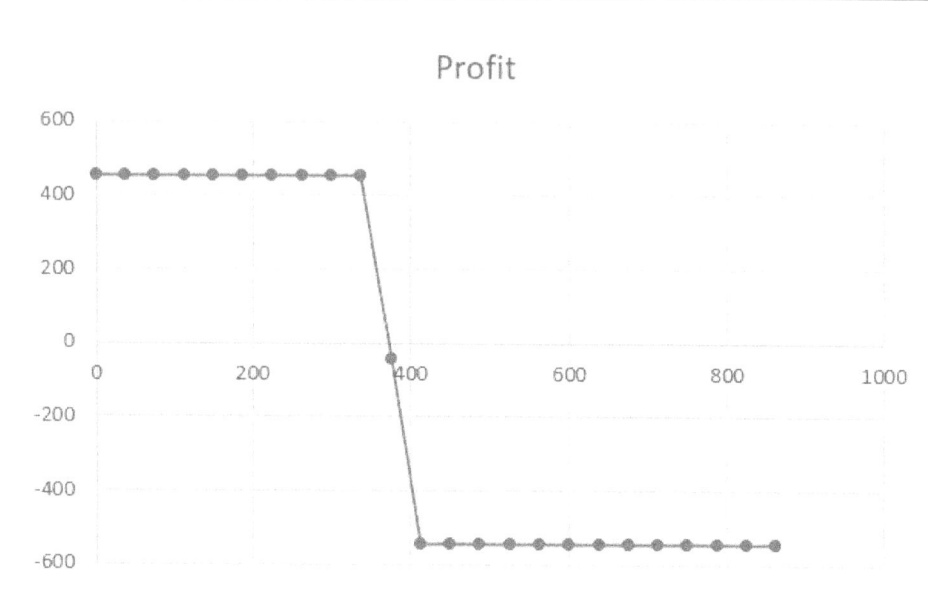

# Vertical Call Spread Option 3

Source: Charles Schwab

Tim owns 300 shares of Palantir stock, and he wants to sell vertical call spreads using information above. He sells a call at a strike price of $25; and buys a call at a strike price of $30.

    i.      What is the net premium that he receives?
    ii.     If after 295 days, Palantir is at $31, what is his profit/loss?
    iii.    What happens if Palantir is at $20 at expiration

# Vertical Call Spread Option 3 (with Answers)

i. What is the net premium that he receives?
ii. If after 295 days, Palantir is at $31, what is his profit/loss?
iii. What happens if Palantir is at $20 at expiration?


i. $470*3 - $310*3 = **$480 Premium**
ii. If Palantir is at $31, he loses on the $25 call. He loses ($31-$25)*300 = $1800 loss
 He gains on the $40 call.
 He gains ($31-$30)*300 = $300. He also gains a premium of $480.
 So, his net loss = $1800 - $300 - $480 = **$1020 loss**
iii. If Palantir is at $20, both call options expires worthless.
 He gains on the premium. So, his **gain is $480** total.

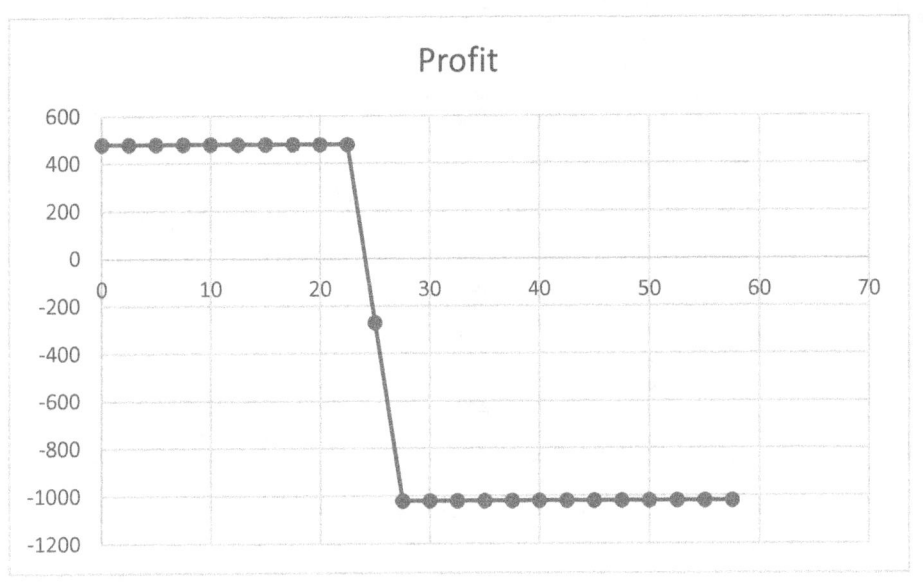

# Vertical Call Spread Option 4

Source: Charles Schwab

Bob owns 100 shares of the SPDR S&P 500, and he wants to sell a vertical call spread using information above. He wants to sell a call option at a strike price of $445 and buy a call option at a strike price of $450.

i. What is the net premium that he receives?
ii. If after 148 days, the stock is at $430, what's his profit

# Vertical Call Spread Option 4 (with Answers)

| Trade | Select | ⓘ | 127 | 11,781 | 18.62 | -1.24 | (18.72) | 18.81 | 445.00 |
|-------|--------|---|-----|--------|-------|-------|---------|-------|--------|
| Trade | Select | ⓘ | 740 | 14,010 | 15.59 | -1.00 | (15.58) | 15.67 | 450.00 |

Bob owns 100 shares of the SPDR S&P 500, and he wants to sell vertical call spread using information above. He wants to sell a call option at a strike price of $445 and buy a call option at a strike price of $450.

    i.      What is the net premium that he receives?
    ii.     If after 148 days, the stock is at $430, what's his profit?


    i.      $1872-$1558 = **$314**
    ii.     Both call options expire worthless. And his profit is equal to the premium of the stock, which is a **profit of $314**

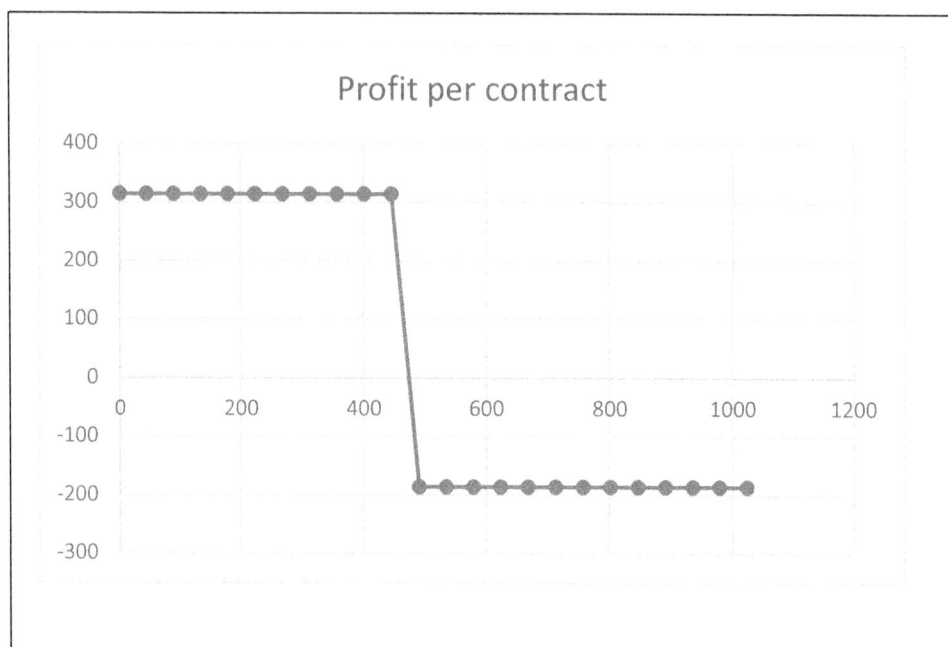

# Vertical Call Spread Option 5

Source: Charles Schwab

Emma owns 100 shares of the General Motors, and he wants to buy a vertical call spread using information above. He plans to sell a call at a strike price of $50 and buy a call at a strike price of $55.

    i.       What is the net premium that she receives?
    ii.      If after 204 days, General Motors is at $50, what is his profit?
    iii.     If General Motors is at $60, what is his profit?

# Vertical Call Spread Option 5 (with Answers)

| Trade | Select | ⓘ | 59 | 2,240 | 4.46 | -0.69 | 4.40 | 4.50 | 50.00 |
| Trade | Select | ⓘ | 40 | 1,342 | 2.71 | -0.39 | 2.65 | 2.71 | 55.00 |

Emma owns 100 shares of the General Motors, and he wants to buy a vertical call spread using information above. He plans to sell a call at a strike price of $50 and buy a call at a strike price of $55.

   i.      What is the net premium that she receives?
   ii.     If after 204 days, General Motors is at $50, what is his profit?
   iii.    If General Motors is at $60, what is his profit?

   i.      $440-$265 = $175 premium
   ii.     His profit is his premium of **$175**.
   iii.    At $60, he loses on the $50 call option. He loses ($60-$50)*100 = $1000. He gains on the $55 call option. He gains ($60-$55)*100 = $500.
           Total loss = $1000 - $500 - $175 = **$325 loss**

# Spread 3 – Vertical Bull Put Spread

## Psychology Behind the Vertical Bull Put Spread

Let's have a look at the example of Sam again. He sells puts in the Chapter titled 'Selling Put Options – Selling Cash Secured Puts'. Sam sells cash secured puts for Apple at a strike price of $50; while Apple is at a price of $100.

Sam receives a premium while waiting for the price of Apple to crash.

The only problem is what happens if Apple crashes to $0?

Sam still has to buy the stock at $50; and loses $5000 per contract. This is a very low probability event for a company like Apple. That's why it's important to pick the right stocks to sell puts on.

However, there is a way to hedge against this possibility.

Sam can buy a put at a lower price, to reduce the downside. So, in this case, Sam can buy a put at $45 with the same expiration date.

So, if the stock falls below $45, Sam can make a profit on the $45 put; which reduces some of his losses from selling the $50 put.

This is called a vertical bull put spread, which is a great way to reduce the risk of selling a put.

## What is a Vertical Bull Put Spread?

A vertical put spread consists of buying a put and selling a put at the same expiration date but with different strike prices. Selling a put is done at a higher strike price with a higher premium. Buying a put is done at a lower strike price so it has a lower premium.

The premium received by selling the put is higher than the premium used for buying the put. So, there is a net positive premium.

# How Vertical Bull Put Spreads Work – An Example

Let's have a look at Tesla stock TSLA. It's a popular stock that has risen a lot. It's currently around $735.72.

| | | | | | | | | | | | | |
|---|---|---|---|---|---|---|---|---|---|---|---|---|
| | | | | | | | | | | | | |

(Options chain table showing TSLA Jun 16, 2023 Calls and Puts across strikes from $260 to $850)

Source: Charles Schwab

You feel that Tesla is overvalued, and you don't want to buy at that price.

You do like the company and would love to buy the company at $300 per share.

So, let's have a look at the put options for Tesla at a strike price of $300.

The premiums cost between $2100 and $2400 per contract of 100 shares. Let's assume that the premium is the minimum in the range.

So, you get paid $2100 to sell the contract. This is called the premium for the put option. Let's assume the premium is $2100.

If the put options drops below $300 any time in the next 653 days, you must buy the stock at a price of $300 per share (or $25000 per contract).

So, you need $30000 to buy Tesla stock when that happens.

The problem happens when Tesla crashes much below $300. What if it falls to 0 and Tesla goes bankrupt?

Then, you pay $300000 for nothing.

To reduce the harm from that happening, you buy a put at a slightly lower price, let's say $250.

## Puts

| Strike | Bid | Ask | Last | Change | Volume | OI | Build | Action |
|---|---|---|---|---|---|---|---|---|
| | | | | | | 42 out of 42 Strikes | Show 8 16 | All |
| 250.00 | 13.25 | 17.25 | 14.50 | 0 | 0 | 409 | Select | Trade |

So, you pay $1325 for the premium.

The net premium is lowered to $775.

So, if the stock falls below $250; you can sell the stock at a price of $250. So $250 is the lower cap on your losses in the event of a crash.

So, let's have a look at 3 different situations that could happen at expiration:

    a. Tesla stock is at $1000
    b. Tesla stock is at $275
    c. Tesla stock is at $100


    a. If Tesla stock is at $1000 per share, both put options expire worthless. So, your profit is equal to the premium of $2100. So the **profit is $775**.

b. If Tesla is at $275, the $250 put option expires worthless. You lose on the $300 put option. You lose ($300-$275)*100 = $2500. But you gain $775 on the premium. So, your **net loss is $1725** ($2500 - $775).
c. If Tesla is at $100, you profit on the $250 option but lose on the $300 option. You profit ($250-$100)*100 = $15000 and also profit the premium of $2100.
You lose ($300-$100)*100 = $20000.
The total loss = $20000 - $15000 - $775 = **$4225 loss**

# Vertical Bull Put Spreads Worksheet

## Vertical Bull Put Spread 1

| | | Calls | | | | | | | Strike | | | Puts | | | | | | |
|---|---|---|---|---|---|---|---|---|---|---|---|---|---|---|---|---|---|---|
| Action | Build | | Volume | OI | Last | Change | Bid | Ask | Strike | Bid | Ask | Last | Change | Volume | OI | | Build | Action |
| WFC Jan 21, 2022 (Fri: 129 days) | | | | | | | | | | | | | | | | 16 out of 25 Strikes Show 0 \| 15 \| All | | |
| Trade | Select | ⓘ | 84 | 22,412 | 18.62 | +0.52 | 18.65 | 18.90 | 27.50 | 0.21 | 0.25 | 0.24 | 0 | 0 | 29,428 | ⓘ | Select | Trade |
| Trade | Select | ⓘ | 55 | 49,222 | 16.25 | +0.25 | 16.25 | 16.45 | 30.00 | 0.30 | 0.34 | 0.33 | +0.01 | 17 | 29,281 | ⓘ | Select | Trade |
| Trade | Select | ⓘ | 445 | 28,402 | 13.95 | +0.50 | 13.85 | 14.10 | 32.50 | 0.44 | 0.49 | 0.46 | -0.01 | 102 | 28,807 | ⓘ | Select | Trade |
| Trade | Select | ⓘ | 50 | 36,219 | 11.57 | +0.22 | 11.50 | 11.75 | 35.00 | 0.65 | 0.69 | 0.67 | -0.02 | 775 | 24,133 | ⓘ | Select | Trade |
| Trade | Select | ⓘ | 25 | 28,082 | 9.41 | +0.41 | 9.40 | 9.55 | 37.50 | 0.96 | 0.99 | 0.99 | +0.01 | 122 | 31,386 | ⓘ | Select | Trade |
| Trade | Select | ⓘ | 186 | 44,950 | 7.35 | +0.20 | 7.35 | 7.50 | 40.00 | 1.43 | 1.45 | 1.45 | -0.02 | 96 | 46,124 | ⓘ | Select | Trade |
| Trade | Select | ⓘ | 619 | 39,268 | 5.60 | +0.30 | 5.50 | 5.85 | 42.50 | 2.09 | 2.15 | 2.19 | 0 | 2,328 | 19,223 | ⓘ | Select | Trade |
| Trade | Select | ⓘ | 465 | 36,557 | 4.08 | +0.28 | 4.00 | 4.10 | 45.00 | 3.05 | 3.15 | 3.10 | -0.10 | 1,393 | 26,451 | ⓘ | Select | Trade |
| Trade | Select | ⓘ | 691 | 26,816 | 2.78 | +0.14 | 2.61 | 2.88 | 47.50 | 4.25 | 4.40 | 4.35 | -0.18 | 52 | 12,681 | ⓘ | Select | Trade |
| Trade | Select | ⓘ | 3,420 | 60,869 | 1.89 | +0.14 | 1.87 | 1.93 | 50.00 | 5.80 | 6.00 | 5.90 | -0.35 | 17 | 13,828 | ⓘ | Select | Trade |

Source: Charles Schwab

Jamie owns 350 shares of Wells Fargo stock (WFC), and he wants to complete a vertical put spread where he sells a put option at $32.5 and buys a put option at $30.

    i.      How many contracts can he sell?
    ii.     What is the net premium that he receives?
    iii.    What happens if Wells Fargo stock is at $35 at expiration?
    iv.    What happens if Wells Fargo stock is at $25 at expiration?

# Vertical Bull Put Spread 1 (Answer)

| | | | | | | | | |
|---|---|---|---|---|---|---|---|---|
| 30.00 | 0.30 | 0.34 | 0.33 | +0.01 | 17 | 29,281 | Select | Trade |
| 32.50 | 0.44 | 0.49 | 0.46 | -0.01 | 102 | 26,807 | Select | Trade |

i. How many contracts can he sell?
ii. What is the net premium that he receives?
iii. What happens if Wells Fargo stock is at $35 at expiration?
iv. What happens if Wells Fargo stock is at $25 at expiration?

i. 3 contracts
ii. Net Premium = (44*3-30*3) = **$42 Premium**
iii. Both put options expire worthless and the profit is the **premium of $42**
iv. Jamie profits on the $30 put option and loses on the $32.5 put option
Jamie's profit on $30 put option = ($30-$25)*100*3 = $1500
Jamie's loss on $32.5 put option = ($32.5-$25)*100*3 = $2250
Jamie also profits on the net premium of $42
Jamie's net loss = 2250 – 1500 – 42 = **$708 loss**

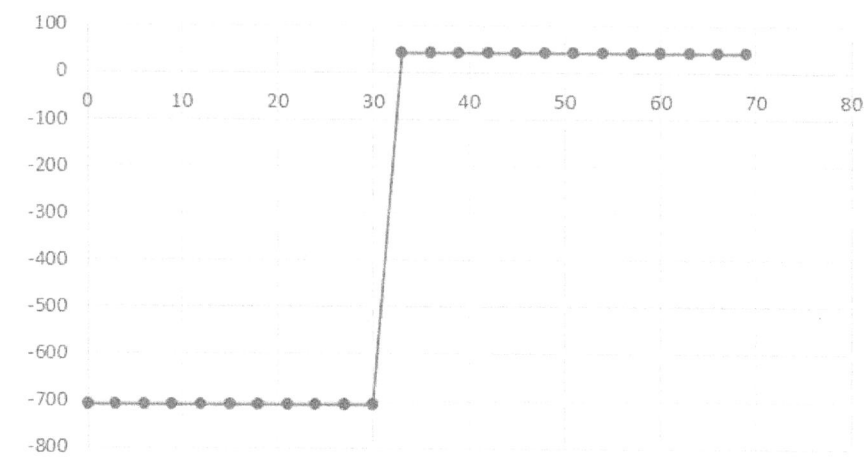

# Vertical Bull Put Spread 2

Steve owns 100 shares of Bank of America (BAC), and he wants to complete a vertical put spread where he sells a put option at $34 and buys a put option at $32.

    i.      What is the net premium that he receives?
    ii.     What happens if Bank of America stock is at $40 at expiration?
    iii.    What happens if Bank of America stock is at $25 at expiration?
    iv.    What happens if Bank of America stock is at $33 at expiration?

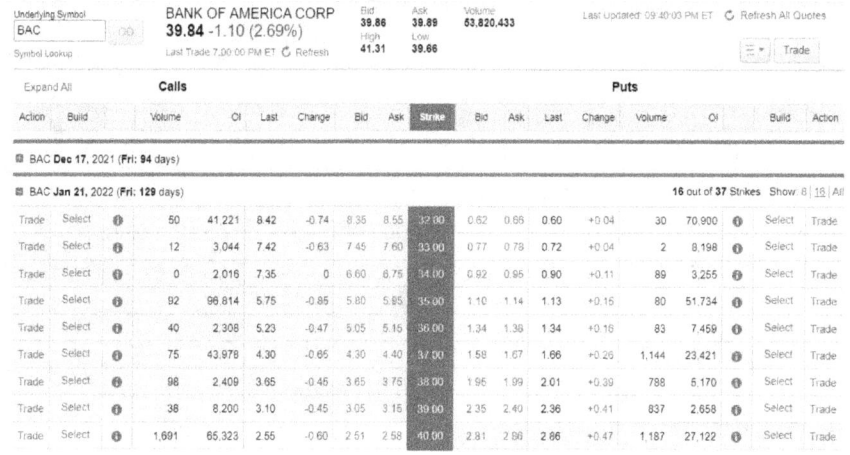

Source: Charles Schwab

# Vertical Bull Put Spread 2 (Answer)

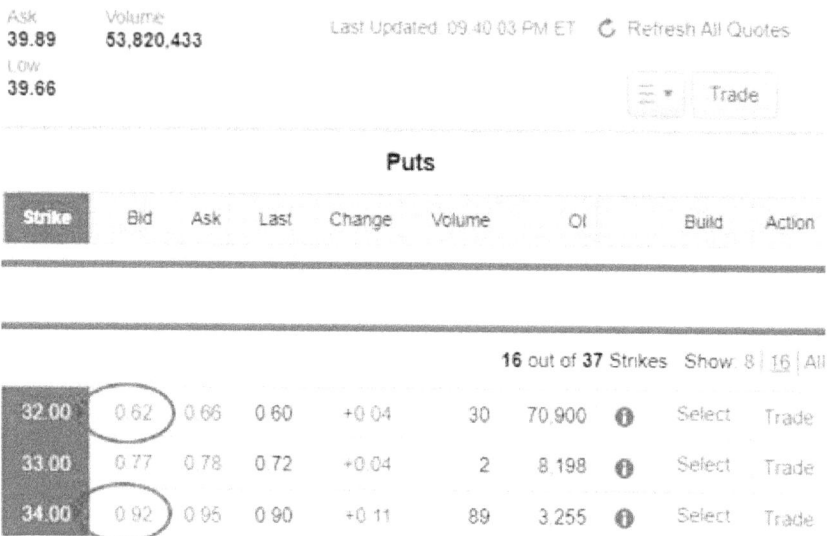

i. What is the net premium that he receives?
ii. What happens if Bank of America stock is at $40 at expiration?
iii. What happens if Bank of America stock is at $25 at expiration?
iv. What happens if Bank of America stock is at $33 at expiration?

i. Net Premium = $92 - $62 = **$30 Premium**
ii. Both put options expire worthless. So, the **net profit is $30 premium.**
iii. Steve gains on the $32 option; and loses on the $34 option
$32 option profit = ($32-$25)*100 = $700
$34 option loss = ($34-$25)*100 = $900
Net Loss = $900 - $700 - $30 = **$170 loss**
iv. The $32 option expires worthless, and Steve loses on the $34 option.
$34 option loss = ($34-$33)*100 = $100
Net Loss = $100 - $30 = **$70 loss**

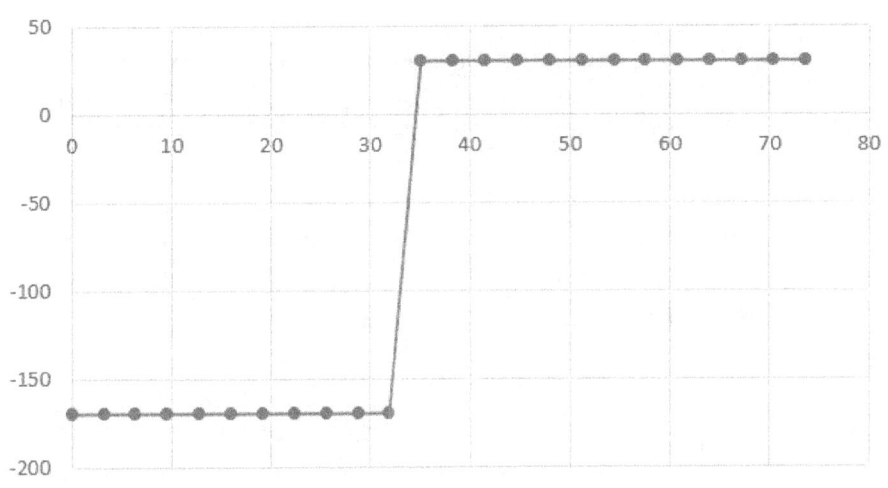

# Vertical Bull Put Spread 3

Wyatt owns 100 shares of Chipotle Mexican grill stock, and he wants to complete a vertical put spread where he sells a put option at $1760 and buys a put option at $1700.

   i.   What is the net premium that he receives?
   ii.  What happens if Chipotle stock is at $1600 at expiration?
   iii. What happens if Chipotle stock is at $1800 at expiration?
   iv.  What happens if Chipotle stock is at $1725 at expiration?

Source: Charles Schwab

# Vertical Bull Put Spread 3 (Answer)

| | Ask | Volume | Last Updated 09:42:07 PM ET | Refresh All Quotes |
|---|---|---|---|---|
| | 1,861.50 | 209,016 | | |
| 01 | Low | | | Trade |
| | 1,849.3199 | | | |

## Puts

| Strike | Bid | Ask | Last | Change | Volume | OI | Build | Action |
|---|---|---|---|---|---|---|---|---|
| | | | | | 16 out of 112 Strikes | | Show 8 \| 16 \| All | |
| 1,700.00 | (45.20) | 48.50 | 50.80 | +4.30 | 21 | 170 | Select | Trade |
| 1,720.00 | 48.70 | 56.40 | 50.60 | +13.50 | 2 | 17 | Select | Trade |
| 1,740.00 | 57.50 | 63.20 | 57.00 | 0 | 9 | 77 | Select | Trade |
| 1,760.00 | (62.10) | 67.90 | 63.06 | 0 | 0 | 26 | Select | Trade |

i. What is the net premium that he receives?
ii. What happens if Chipotle stock is at $1600 at expiration?
iii. What happens if Chipotle stock is at $1800 at expiration?
iv. What happens if Chipotle stock is at $1725 at expiration?

i. Net Premium = $6210 - $4520 = **$1690**
ii. Wyatt gains on the $1700 option, and loses on the $1760 option
$1700 option gain = (1700-1600)*100 = $10000
$1760 option loss = (1760-1600)*100 = $16000
Net loss = $16000 - $10000 - $1690 = **$4310 loss**
iii. Both put options expire worthless. So, the **net profit is the premium of $1690**
iv. The $1700 put option expires worthless. Wyatt loses on the $1760 put option.
$1760 option loss = ($1760 - $1725)*100 = $3500
Net loss = $3500 - $1690 = **$1810 loss**

# Vertical Bull Put Spread 4

Alice owns 100 shares of Apple stock (AAPL), and he wants to complete a vertical put spread where he sells a put option at $135 and buys a put option at $125.

Fill in chart below that shows the net profit vs different stock prices at expiration.

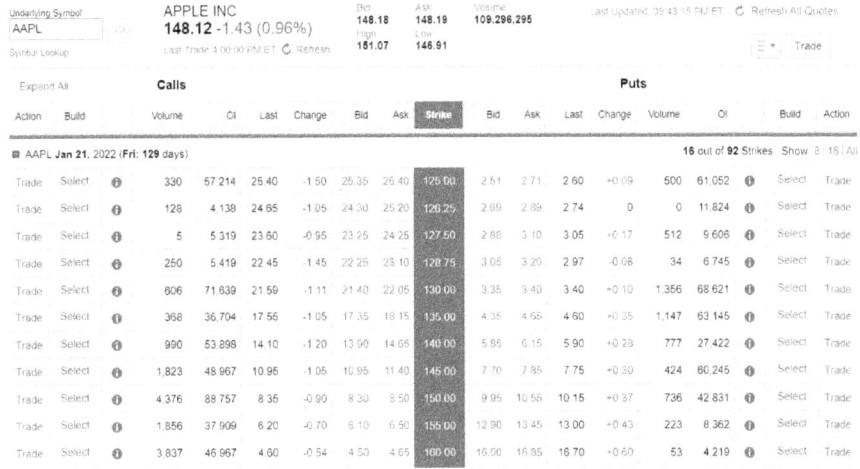

Source: Charles Schwab

# Vertical Bull Put Spread 4 (Answer)

Ask: **148.19**  Volume: **109,296,295**  Last Updated: 09:43:15 PM ET  ℃ Refresh All Quotes
Low: **146.91**

Trade

## Puts

| Strike | Bid | Ask | Last | Change | Volume | OI | | Build | Action |
|---|---|---|---|---|---|---|---|---|---|
| | | | | | | 16 out of 92 Strikes | | Show: 8 \| 16 \| All | |
| 125.00 | 2.51 | 2.71 | 2.60 | +0.09 | 500 | 61,052 | ⓘ | Select | Trade |
| 126.25 | 2.69 | 2.89 | 2.74 | 0 | 0 | 11,824 | ⓘ | Select | Trade |
| 127.50 | 2.88 | 3.10 | 3.05 | +0.17 | 512 | 9,606 | ⓘ | Select | Trade |
| 128.75 | 3.05 | 3.20 | 2.97 | -0.08 | 34 | 6,745 | ⓘ | Select | Trade |
| 130.00 | 3.35 | 3.40 | 3.40 | +0.10 | 1,356 | 68,621 | ⓘ | Select | Trade |
| 135.00 | 4.35 | 4.65 | 4.60 | +0.35 | 1,147 | 63,145 | ⓘ | Select | Trade |

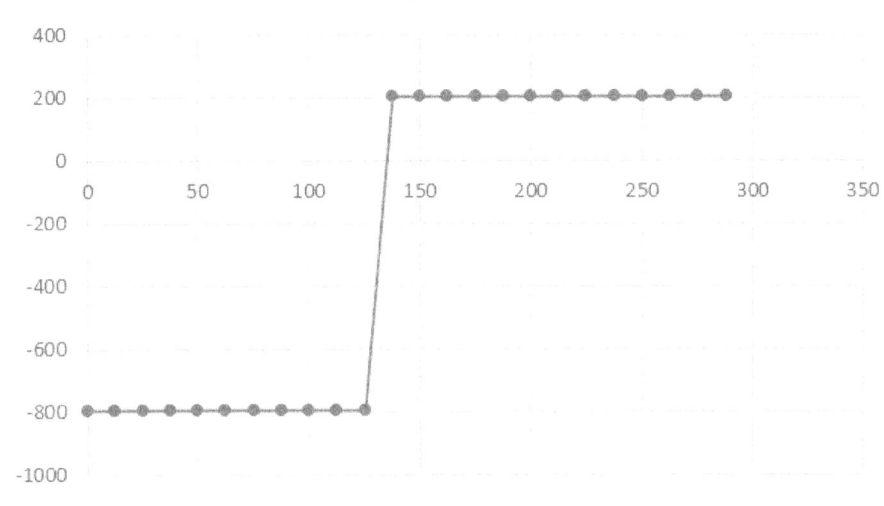

# Vertical Bull Put Spread 5

Steve owns 100 shares of Delta Airlines (DAL), and he wants to complete a vertical put spread where he sells a put option at $38 and buys a put option at $34.

    i.       What is the net premium that he receives?

    ii.      Draw a chart that shows the net profit vs different stock prices at expiration

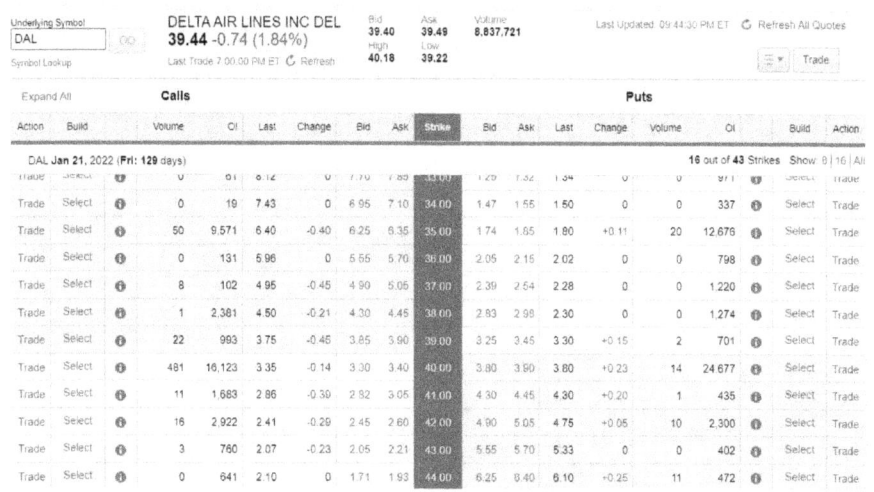

Source: Charles Schwab

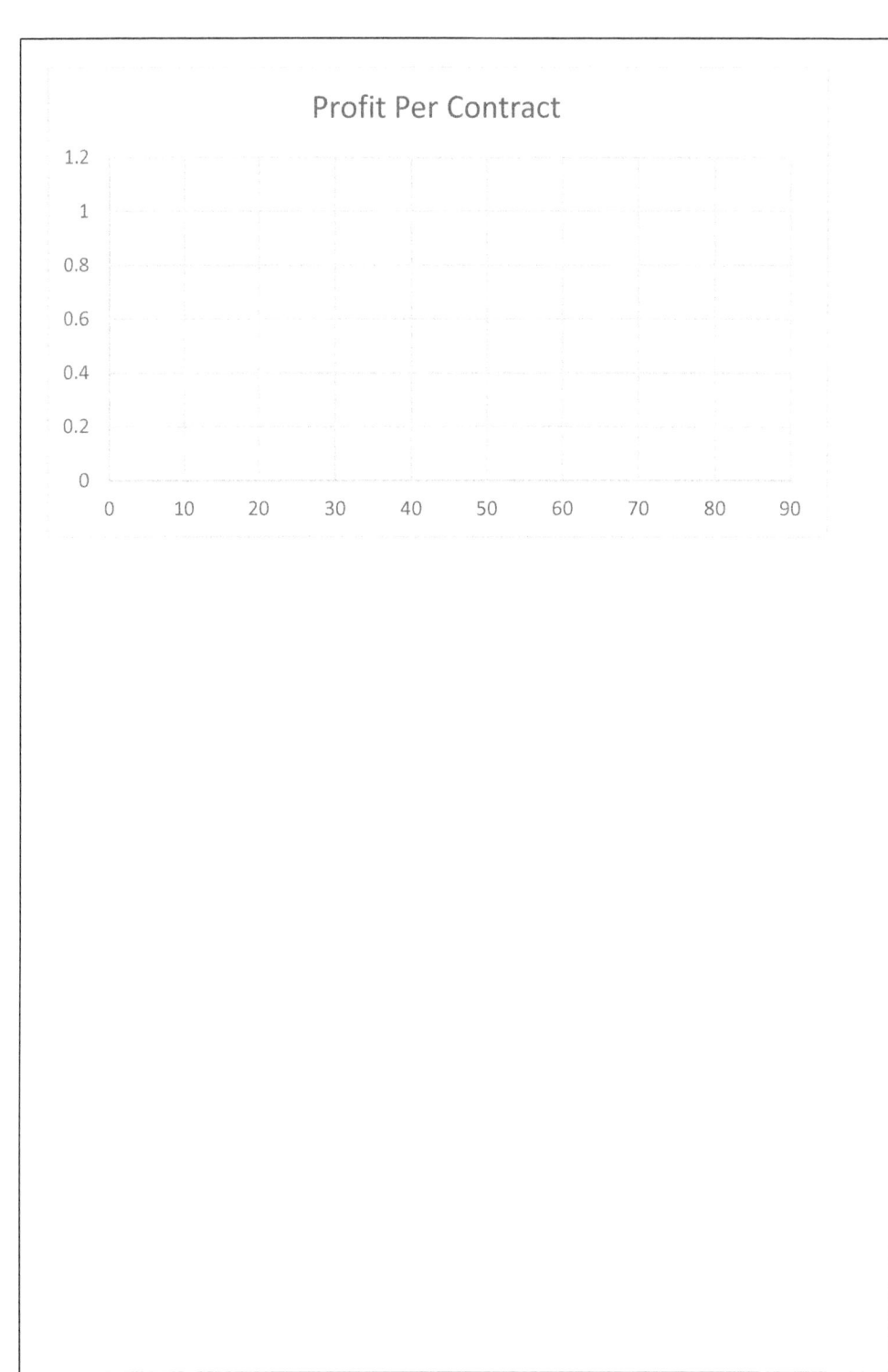

# Vertical Bull Put Spread 5 (Answer)

| Strike | Bid | Ask | Mid | Change | Vol | OI | | Action | |
|---|---|---|---|---|---|---|---|---|---|
| 34.00 | 1.47 | 1.55 | 1.50 | 0 | 0 | 337 | ⓘ | Select | Trade |
| 35.00 | 1.74 | 1.85 | 1.80 | +0.11 | 20 | 12,676 | ⓘ | Select | Trade |
| 36.00 | 2.05 | 2.15 | 2.02 | 0 | 0 | 798 | ⓘ | Select | Trade |
| 37.00 | 2.39 | 2.54 | 2.28 | 0 | 0 | 1,220 | ⓘ | Select | Trade |
| 38.00 | 2.83 | 2.98 | 2.30 | 0 | 0 | 1,274 | ⓘ | Select | Trade |

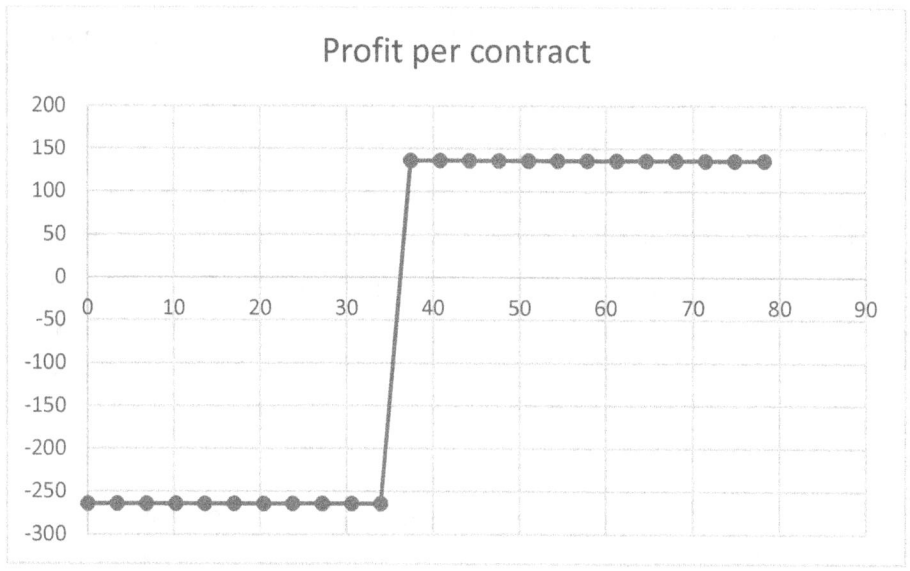

# Spread 4 – Iron Condor

## Psychology Behind the Iron Condor

Jonathan has been holding Verizon stock for the last five years. The stock hasn't moved much through one of the most volatile periods in stock market history. Verizon is a very stable business with consistent revenue from it's customers. It's got a consistent dividend and a strong moat around it's competitors.

Jonathan has been learning different options strategies the last few years. He doesn't want to do any options for Verizon as he doesn't expect it to move too much from it's current price. He would be surprised if it moved too much.

Then, he learnt about Iron Condors.

Iron Condors let Jonathan make a premium when the stock stays within a price range at expiration. The lower the price range, the higher the premium.

He invested in an Iron Condor for Verizon with a high range that he thought Verizon would never cross. He received a premium each time Verizon expired within the range. He bought another Iron Condor after expiration; and kept repeating the process to get more premiums.

## What is an Iron Condor?

An iron condor involves buying two spreads with the same expiration date on the same stock. The first spread is a vertical bear call spread; and the second is a vertical bull put spread.

One receives a premium from both spreads. So, the net premium received is a combined total of both premiums.

# How Iron Condors Work – An Example

Jonathan buys an iron condor for Verizon stock that expires on July 15$^{th}$, 2022.

He buys a vertical bear call spread with call strikes at $60 and $65.

He buys a vertical bull put spread with put strikes at $45 and $50.

| | | | | Calls | | | | Strike | | | Puts | | | | | |
|---|---|---|---|---|---|---|---|---|---|---|---|---|---|---|---|---|
| Action | Build | Volume | OI | Last | Change | Bid | Ask | Strike | Bid | Ask | Last | Change | Volume | OI | Build | Action |
| Trade | Select | 0 | 3 | 24.77 | 0 | 24.45 | 24.80 | 30.00 | 0.19 | 0.25 | 0.21 | 0 | 0 | 47 | Select | Trade |
| Trade | Select | 0 | 0 | 0.00 | 0 | 19.50 | 20.05 | 35.00 | 0.27 | 0.34 | 0.30 | 0 | 0 | 24 | Select | Trade |
| Trade | Select | 0 | 5 | 14.93 | 0 | 14.45 | 14.70 | 40.00 | 0.50 | 0.56 | 0.53 | 0 | 0 | 389 | Select | Trade |
| Trade | Select | 0 | 78 | 9.55 | 0 | 9.50 | 9.80 | 45.00 | 1.00 | 1.06 | 1.00 | 0 | 0 | 317 | Select | Trade |
| Trade | Select | 0 | 227 | 5.29 | 0 | 5.20 | 5.30 | 50.00 | 2.16 | 2.24 | 2.13 | 0 | 0 | 1,193 | Select | Trade |
| Trade | Select | 0 | 217 | 3.62 | 0 | 3.55 | 3.65 | 52.50 | 3.15 | 3.30 | 3.13 | 0 | 0 | 1,296 | Select | Trade |
| Trade | Select | 0 | 580 | 2.35 | 0 | 2.33 | 2.40 | 55.00 | 4.55 | 4.70 | 4.70 | 0 | 0 | 307 | Select | Trade |
| Trade | Select | 0 | 1,853 | 1.43 | 0 | 1.50 | 1.57 | 57.50 | 6.30 | 6.45 | 6.30 | 0 | 0 | 133 | Select | Trade |
| Trade | Select | 0 | 578 | 0.98 | 0 | 0.96 | 1.02 | 60.00 | 8.30 | 8.45 | 8.53 | 0 | 0 | 55 | Select | Trade |
| Trade | Select | 0 | 752 | 0.66 | 0 | 0.62 | 0.87 | 62.50 | 10.50 | 10.65 | 10.70 | 0 | 0 | 6 | Select | Trade |
| Trade | Select | 0 | 142 | 0.44 | 0 | 0.41 | 0.47 | 65.00 | 12.80 | 12.95 | 12.40 | 0 | 0 | 28 | Select | Trade |
| Trade | Select | 0 | 467 | 0.25 | 0 | 0.23 | 0.29 | 70.00 | 16.80 | 18.80 | 16.65 | 0 | 0 | 1 | Select | Trade |
| Trade | Select | 0 | 162 | 0.18 | 0 | 0.16 | 0.25 | 75.00 | 21.90 | 23.40 | 0.00 | 0 | 0 | 0 | Select | Trade |
| Trade | Select | 0 | 299 | 0.16 | 0 | 0.13 | 0.25 | 80.00 | 26.70 | 28.40 | 0.00 | 0 | 0 | 0 | Select | Trade |

Source: Charles Schwab

## Iron Condor Part 1 – Vertical Bear Call Spread

| Trade | Select | 0 | 578 | 0.98 | 0 | 0.96 | 1.02 | 60.00 |
|---|---|---|---|---|---|---|---|---|
| Trade | Select | 0 | 752 | 0.66 | 0 | 0.62 | 0.67 | 62.50 |
| Trade | Select | 0 | 142 | 0.44 | 0 | 0.41 | 0.47 | 65.00 |

He sells a call at $60. So, he receives $96 in premium.

He buys a call at $65. So, he pays a premium of $41.

His net premium on this part of the iron condor is **$55** ($96-$41)

Iron Condor Part 2 – Vertical Bull Put Spread

| 45.00 | 1.00 | 1.06 | 1.00 | 0 | 0 | 317 | | Select | Trade |
|---|---|---|---|---|---|---|---|---|---|
| 50.00 | 2.16 | 2.24 | 2.13 | 0 | 0 | 1,193 | | Select | Trade |

He sells a put at $50. So he receives $216 in premium.

He buys a put at $45. So, he pays a premium of $100.

His net premium on this part of the iron condor is **$116** ($216-$100)

So, Iron Condor net premium = $116+$55 = **$171 premium**


Now, let's look at 5 different situations when the Iron Condor expires:

a. Verizon stock is at $55 at expiration
b. Verizon stock is at $70 at expiration
c. Verizon stock is at $35 at expiration
d. Verizon stock is at $47 at expiration
e. Verizon stock is at $63 at expiration

a. If Verizon stock is at $55, all 4 options are worthless at expiration. So, his profit is the net premium. His **profit is $171**.
b. If Verizon stock is at $70, the two put options expire worthless. He makes a profit on the $65 call option, and a loss on the $60 call option.
   He makes ($70-$65)*100=$500 profit on the $70 call
   He loses ($70-$60)*100=$1000 loss on the $60 call
   So, his net loss = $1000 - $500 - $171 = **$329 Loss**
c. If Verizon stock is at $35, the two call options expire worthless. He makes a profit on the $45 put option, and a loss on the $50 call option.
   He makes ($45-$35)*100=$1000 profit on the $45 call
   He loses ($50-$35)*100=$1500 loss on the $50 call
   So, his net loss = $1500 - $1000 - $171 = **$329 Loss**
d. If Verizon stock is at $47, the two call options expire worthless. He makes a loss on the $50 put option, and the $45 put option expires worthless.
   He loses ($50-$47)*100=$300 loss on the $50 call
   So, his net loss = $300 - $171 = **$129 Loss**
e. If Verizon stock is at $63, the two call options expire worthless. He makes a loss on the $60 call option, and the $65 call option expires worthless.
   He loses ($63-$60)*100=$300 loss on the $50 call
   So, his net loss = $300 - $171 = **$129 Loss**

Above is a chart of the iron condor. If the stock expires between the strike prices, he receives a premium of $171.

If the stock is outside of the strike price ranges at expiration, he makes a consistent loss of $329.

# Iron Condor Spreads Worksheet

## Iron Condor 1

| | Calls | | | | | | Strike | Puts | | | | | | |
|---|---|---|---|---|---|---|---|---|---|---|---|---|---|---|
| Action | Build | | Volume | OI | Last | Change | Bid | Ask | Strike | Bid | Ask | Last | Change | Volume | OI | Build | Action |

AAPL Jun 17, 2022 (Fri: 273 days)

| Trade | Select | 65 | 16,452 | 31.30 | -1.65 | 31.15 | 31.35 | 120.00 | 5.20 | 5.30 | 5.28 | +0.58 | 36 | 20,490 | Select | Trade |
|---|---|---|---|---|---|---|---|---|---|---|---|---|---|---|---|---|
| Trade | Select | 110 | 7,190 | 30.85 | -2.43 | 30.15 | 30.40 | 121.25 | 5.50 | 5.60 | 5.55 | +0.40 | 15 | 3,438 | Select | Trade |
| Trade | Select | 23 | 4,881 | 29.40 | -1.05 | 29.20 | 29.40 | 122.50 | 5.75 | 5.90 | 5.80 | +0.80 | 60 | 2,628 | Select | Trade |
| Trade | Select | 37 | 9,832 | 27.45 | -2.06 | 27.30 | 27.55 | 125.00 | 6.40 | 6.50 | 6.45 | +0.45 | 129 | 14,662 | Select | Trade |
| Trade | Select | 33 | 9,736 | 23.90 | -1.92 | 23.75 | 23.95 | 130.00 | 7.60 | 7.90 | 7.80 | +0.45 | 617 | 11,420 | Select | Trade |
| Trade | Select | 79 | 11,318 | 20.45 | -1.70 | 20.45 | 20.60 | 135.00 | 9.45 | 9.60 | 9.52 | +0.62 | 94 | 11,124 | Select | Trade |
| Trade | Select | 87 | 28,841 | 17.59 | -1.61 | 17.45 | 17.60 | 140.00 | 11.45 | 11.60 | 11.48 | +1.08 | 248 | 6,920 | Select | Trade |
| Trade | Select | 200 | 13,577 | 14.95 | -1.34 | 14.80 | 14.95 | 145.00 | 13.75 | 13.90 | 13.80 | +1.23 | 249 | 9,334 | Select | Trade |
| Trade | Select | 594 | 22,162 | 12.55 | -1.25 | 12.45 | 12.60 | 150.00 | 16.40 | 16.55 | 16.35 | +1.20 | 193 | 6,584 | Select | Trade |
| Trade | Select | 358 | 12,489 | 10.50 | -1.20 | 10.40 | 10.55 | 155.00 | 19.35 | 19.50 | 19.30 | +1.45 | 8 | 3,333 | Select | Trade |
| Trade | Select | 847 | 22,084 | 8.72 | -0.98 | 8.65 | 8.80 | 160.00 | 22.60 | 22.80 | 22.22 | +0.57 | 373 | 1,887 | Select | Trade |
| Trade | Select | 134 | 10,251 | 7.30 | -0.80 | 7.20 | 7.35 | 165.00 | 26.10 | 26.30 | 24.90 | 0 | 0 | 726 | Select | Trade |
| Trade | Select | 110 | 16,079 | 6.00 | -0.75 | 5.95 | 6.10 | 170.00 | 29.85 | 30.05 | 29.44 | +1.59 | 2 | 1,145 | Select | Trade |

Source: Charles Schwab

Abhi purchases an iron condor for Apple that expires on June 17, 2022.

The put strike prices are $130 and $135; while the call strike prices are $165 and $170.

   a. What is the net premium he receives?
   b. What happens if Apple expires at $150?
   c. What happens if Apple expires at $125?
   d. What happens if Apple expires at $166?

| 130.00 | 7.80 | 7.90 | 7.80 | +0.45 | 617 | 11,420 | ⓘ | Select | Trade |
| 135.00 | 9.45 | 9.60 | 9.52 | +0.62 | 94 | 11,124 | ⓘ | Select | Trade |

Net Premium on Puts = $945-$780 = $165

| Trade | Select | ⓘ | 134 | 10,251 | 7.30 | -0.80 | 7.20 | 7.35 | 165.00 |
| Trade | Select | ⓘ | 110 | 16,079 | 6.00 | -0.75 | 5.95 | 6.10 | 170.00 |

Net Premium on Calls = $720-$595 = $125

a. Net Premium on Iron Condor = $165+$125 = **$290**
b. If Apple expires at $150, all 4 options expire worthless, and Abhi's profit is the premium of **$290.**
c. If Apple expires at $125, both call options expire worthless. Abhi makes money on selling the $135 put, and loses money on buying the $130 put.
Loss on Selling the $135 Put = (135-125)*100 = $1000
Profit on Selling the $130 Put = (130-125)*100 = $500
Net Loss = $1000 - $500 - $290 (Premium) = **$210 Loss**
d. If Apple expires at $166, both put options expire worthless. Abhi makes money on the $165 call, and loses money on the $170 call.
Loss on Selling the $170 call = (170-166)*100 = $400
Profit on Buying the $165 call = (166-165)*100 = $100
Net Loss = $400-$100-$290 = **$10 Loss**

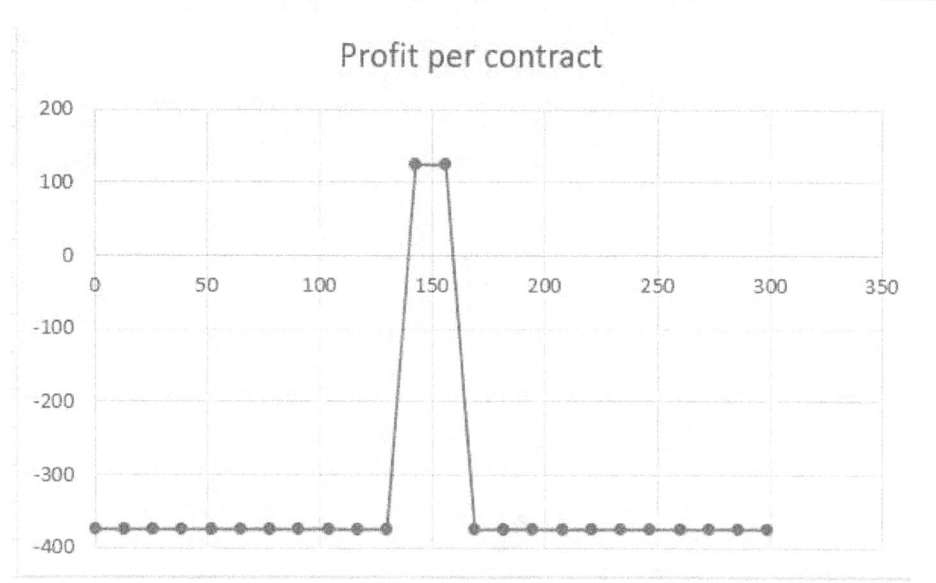

# Iron Condor 2

Source: Charles Schwab

Jenny purchases an iron condor for AT&T that expires in 35 days.

The put strike prices are $22 and $24; while the call strike prices are $31 and $33.

    a. What is the net premium he receives?
    b. What happens if AT&T expires at $25?
    c. What happens if AT&T expires at $12?
    d. What happens if AT&T expires at $18?
    e. What happens if AT&T expires at $45?

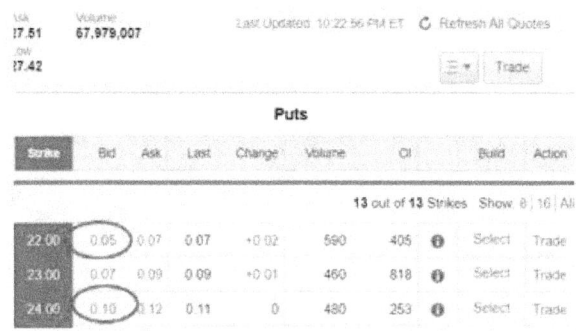

Net Premium on Puts = $10-$5 = $5

Net Premium on Calls = $3 - $0 = $3

| Trade | Select | | 57 | 130 | 0.04 | +0.01 | 0.03 | 0.04 | 31.00 |
| Trade | Select | | 0 | 28 | 0.04 | 0 | 0.00 | 0.10 | 32.00 |
| Trade | Select | | 24 | 110 | 0.03 | 0 | 0.00 | 0.03 | 33.00 |

Net Premium = $5 + $3 = **$8**

a. All 4 options expire worthless. The **profit is the net premium of $8**
b. Both call options expire worthless. Jenny makes a profit on the $22 put option, and a loss on the $24 put option.
   Jenny profit on $22 put option = ($22-$12)*100 = $1000
   Jenny loss on $24 put option = ($24-$12)*100 = $1200
   Net loss = $1200 - $1000 - $8 = **$192 loss**
c. Both call options expire worthless. Jenny makes a profit on the $22 put option, and a loss on the $24 put option.
   Jenny profit on $22 put option = ($22-$18)*100 = $400
   Jenny loss on $24 put option = ($24-$18)*100 = $600
   Net loss = $600 - $400 - $8 = **$192 loss**
d. Both put options expire worthless. Jenny makes a profit on the $33 call option, and a loss on the $31 call option.
   Jenny profit on $33 call option = ($45-$33)*100 = $1200
   Jenny loss on $31 call option = ($45-$31)*100 = $1400
   Net loss = $1400 - $1200 - $8 = **$192 loss**

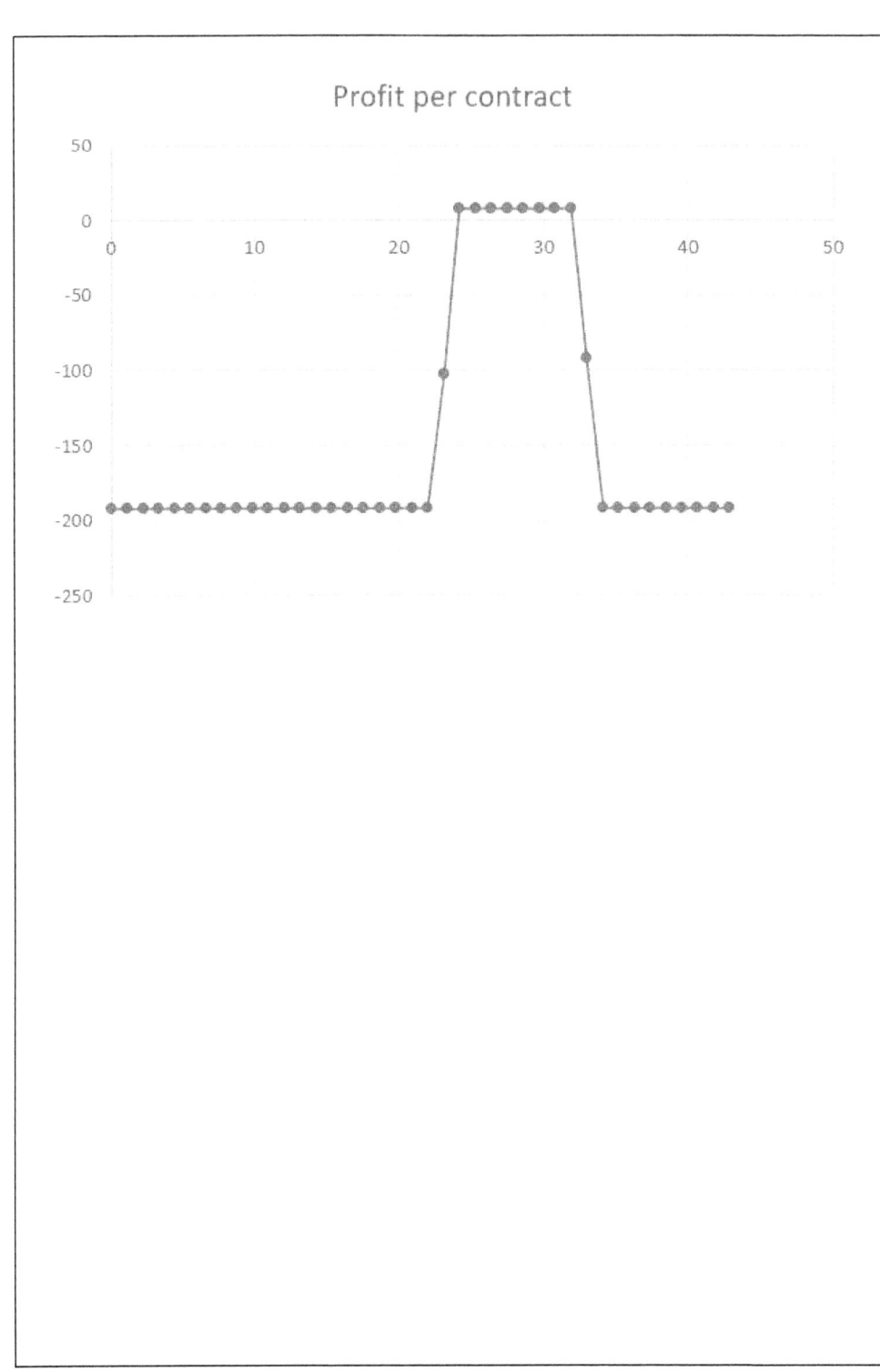

# Iron Condor 3

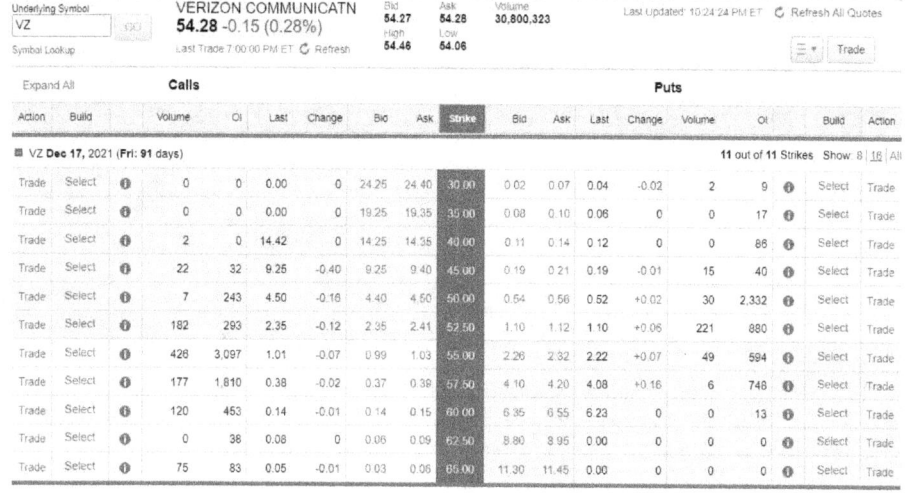

Source: Charles Schwab

Tom purchases an iron condor for Verizon that expires in 91 days.

The put strike prices are $35 and $40; while the call strike prices are $60 and $65.

Estimate the net premium received and draw a chart of price at expiration vs profit for the options contract

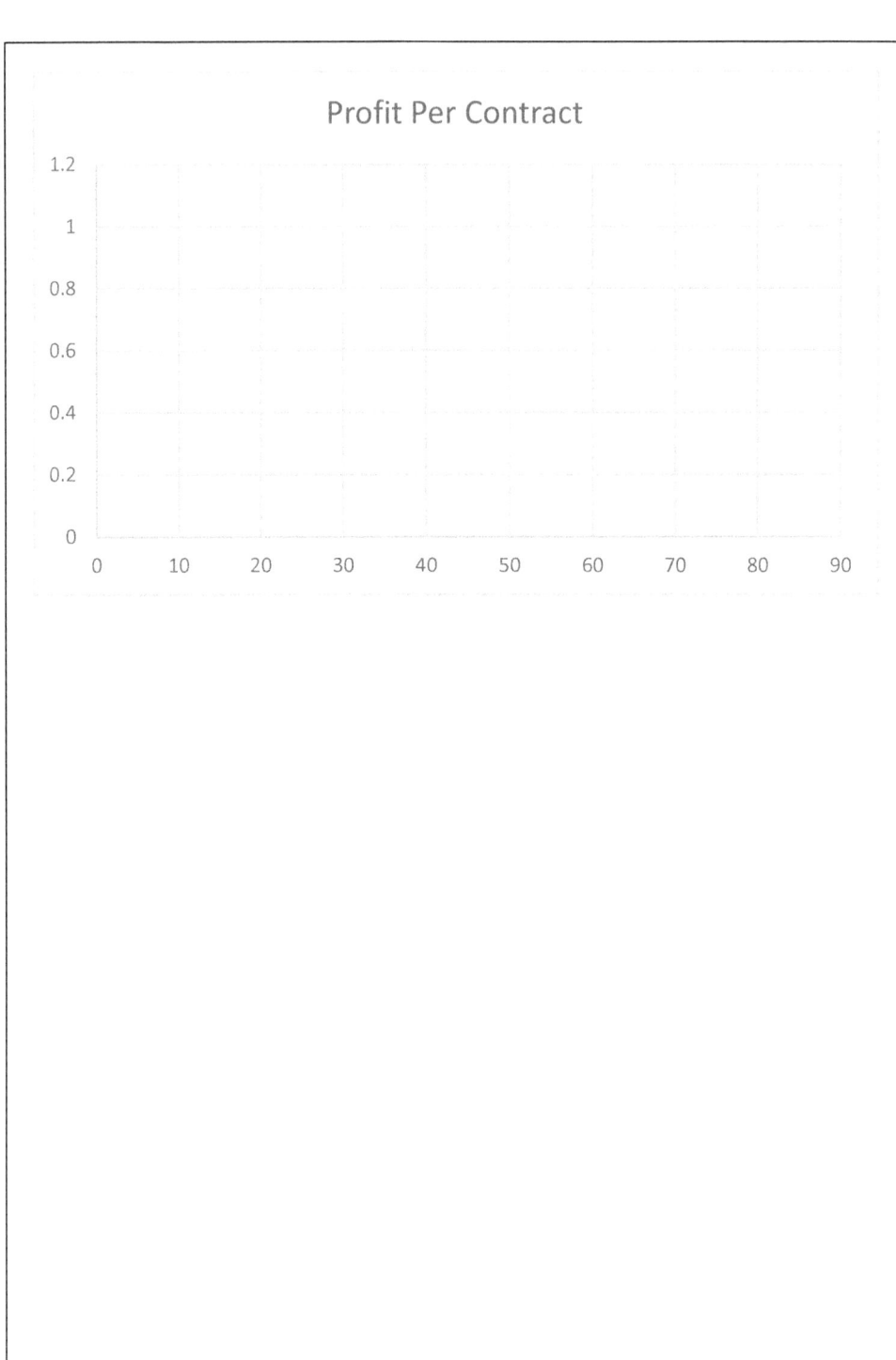

| | | | | | | | | | |
|---|---|---|---|---|---|---|---|---|---|
| 35.00 | 0.08 | 0.10 | 0.06 | 0 | 0 | 17 | ⓘ | Select | Trade |
| 40.00 | 0.11 | 0.14 | 0.12 | 0 | 0 | 86 | ⓘ | Select | Trade |
| 45.00 | 0.19 | 0.21 | 0.19 | -0.01 | 15 | 40 | ⓘ | Select | Trade |

| | | | | | | | | | |
|---|---|---|---|---|---|---|---|---|---|
| Trade | Select | ⓘ | 120 | 453 | 0.14 | -0.01 | 0.14 | 0.15 | 60.00 |
| Trade | Select | ⓘ | 0 | 38 | 0.08 | 0 | 0.06 | 0.09 | 62.50 |
| Trade | Select | ⓘ | 75 | 83 | 0.05 | -0.01 | 0.03 | 0.06 | 65.00 |

Premium on calls = $14-$3=$11

Premium on puts = $19-$8=$7

Net Premium = $11+$7 = $18 net premium

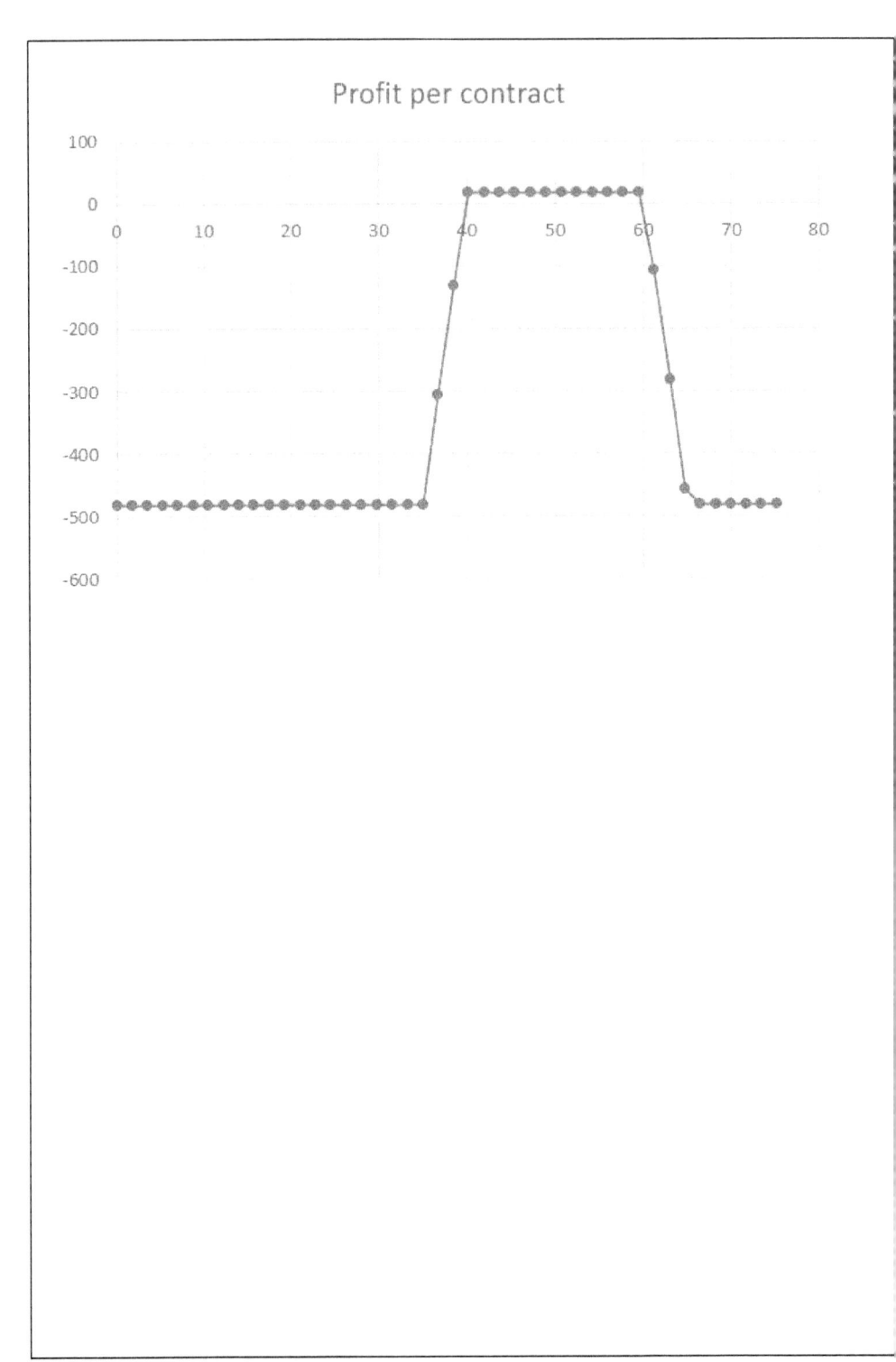

# Iron Condor 4

Source: Charles Schwab

Steve purchases an iron condor for Facebook that expires in 364 days.

The put strike prices are $340 and $345; while the call strike prices are $395 and $400.

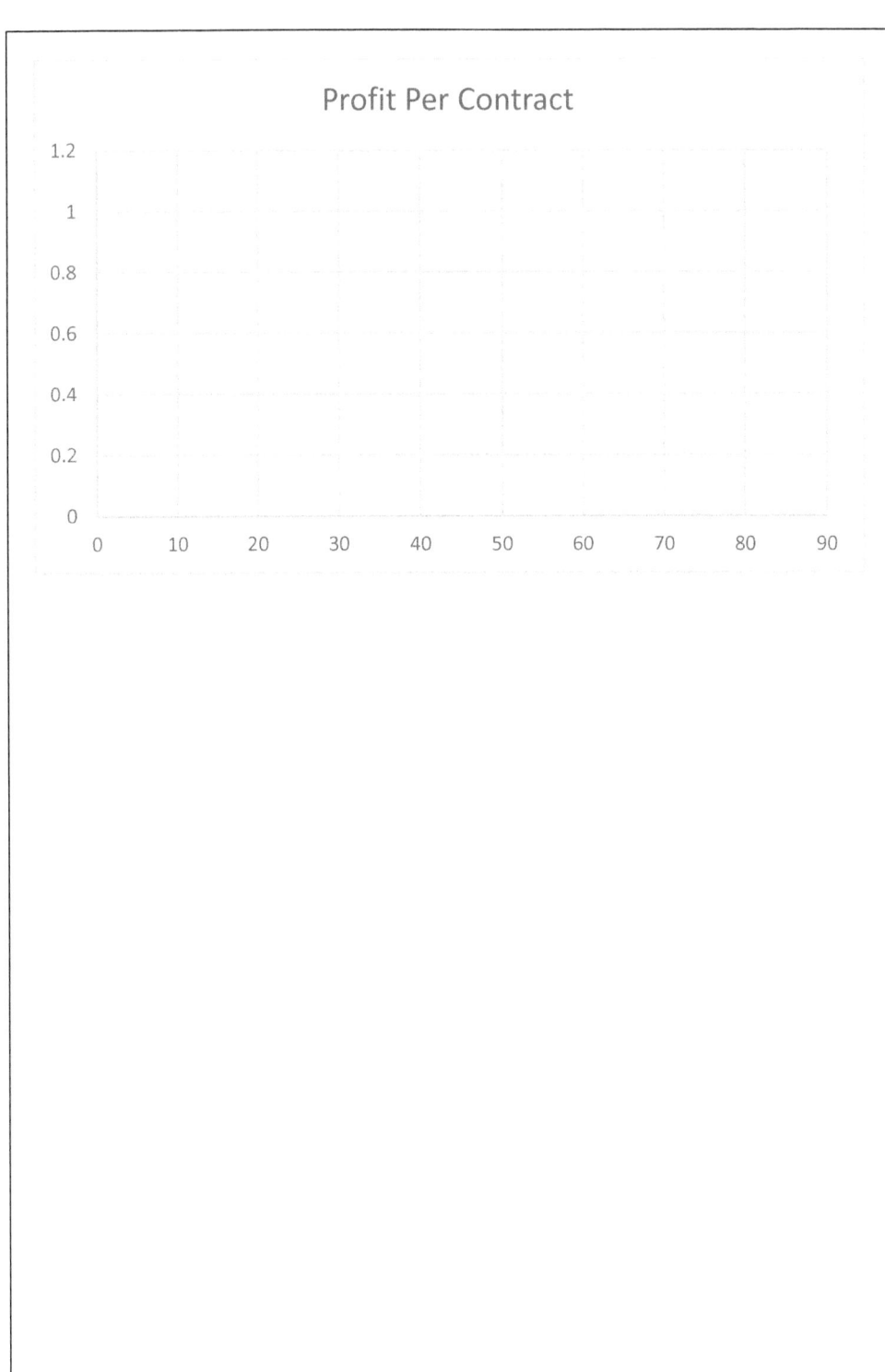

| 340.00 | 33.40 | 34.00 | 34.35 | +2.40 | 13 | 732 | ⓘ | Select | Trade |
| 345.00 | 33.70 | 37.65 | 36.35 | +2.45 | 1 | 198 | ⓘ | Select | Trade |

| Trade | Select | ⓘ | 2 | 1,232 | 33.00 | -3.88 | 31.25 | 35.50 | 395.00 |
| Trade | Select | ⓘ | 12 | 1,561 | 30.40 | -4.01 | 31.05 | 32.95 | 400.00 |

Premium on puts = $3370-$3340 = $30

Premium on calls = $3125 - $3105 = $20

Net Premium = $30 + $20 = $50

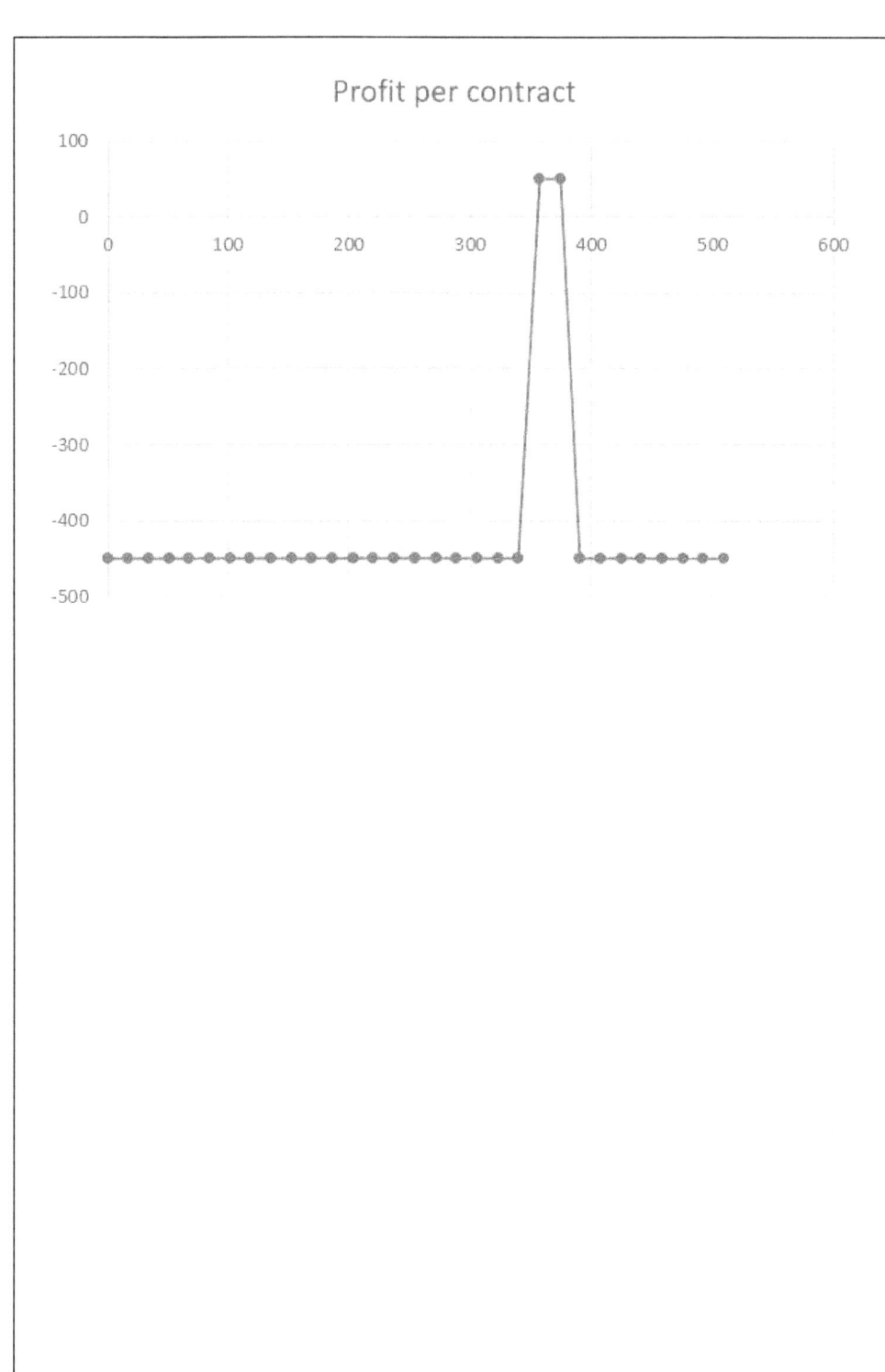

# Iron Condor 5

Source: Charles Schwab

Wells purchases an iron condor for Amazon that expires in 28 days.

The put strike prices are $3400 and $3450; while the call strike prices are $3600 and $3650.

| | | | | | | | | | |
|---|---|---|---|---|---|---|---|---|---|
| 3,400.00 | 52.40 | 54.40 | 53.71 | +11.11 | 825 | 4,085 | ⓘ | Select | Trade |
| 3,410.00 | 55.65 | 57.65 | 58.00 | +11.20 | 93 | 301 | ⓘ | Select | Trade |
| 3,420.00 | 59.00 | 61.15 | 61.50 | +8.15 | 23 | 185 | ⓘ | Select | Trade |
| 3,430.00 | 62.60 | 64.80 | 65.73 | +14.36 | 25 | 249 | ⓘ | Select | Trade |
| 3,440.00 | 66.40 | 68.90 | 69.04 | +12.49 | 48 | 535 | ⓘ | Select | Trade |
| 3,450.00 | 70.40 | 72.85 | 72.01 | +14.01 | 384 | 968 | ⓘ | Select | Trade |

| | | | | | | | | | |
|---|---|---|---|---|---|---|---|---|---|
| Trade | Select | ⓘ | 4,966 | 14,127 | 24.40 | -4.60 | 24.00 | 25.05 | 3,600.00 |
| Trade | Select | ⓘ | 321 | 1,634 | 15.55 | -2.50 | 14.60 | 15.65 | 3,650.00 |
| Trade | Select | ⓘ | 1,761 | 8,702 | 9.70 | -1.10 | 9.20 | 9.90 | 3,700.00 |

Premium on calls = $7040 - $5240 = $1800

Premium on puts = $2400 - $1460 = $940

Net premium = $1800 + $940 = $2740

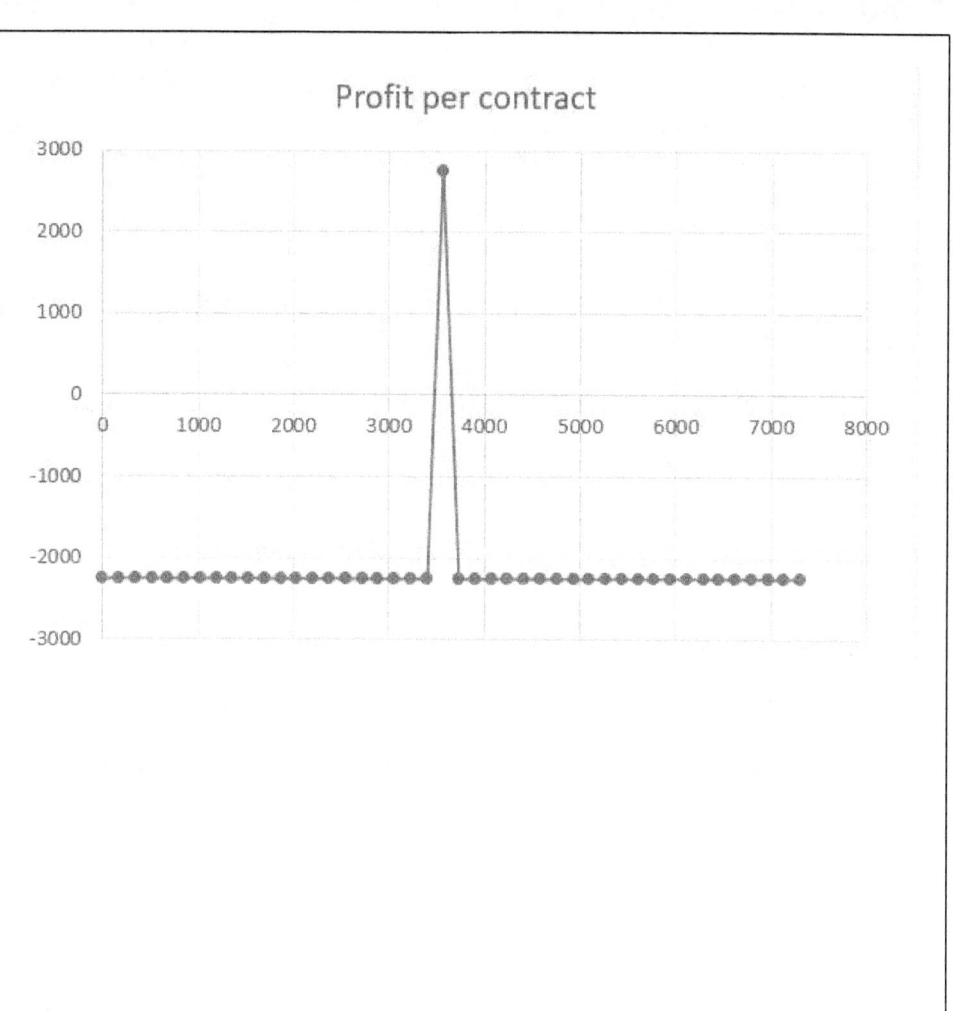

# Use of Volatility

## What is Volatility?

Volatility of a stock is a measure of the fluctuation in the price of a stock.

A highly volatile stocks has more swings in price in both directions; and less predictable.

A low volatile stock is more static and has less frequent changes in price. It is more predictable.

## What is Implied Volatility?

Implied volatility is a common term used in Options Trading.

Implied volatility is the estimate of the future volatility of the stock, based on several factors, including 1 year volatility history of the stock.

Implied volatility is used to determine prices of options for a stock.

A high implied volatility means higher call and put option prices. This asserts that it cost more to buy call and put options for a stock with high implied volatility.

A low implied volatility means lower call and put option prices. This asserts that it cost less to buy call and put options for a stock with high implied volatility.

## What is IV Rank?

The problem with Implied volatility is that it is purely a measure of the individual stock. If a stock is always volatile, the implied volatility will always be high; and it is hard to determine when is the best time to trade options.

It's important to figure out when the stock has a high/low implied volatility relative to it's own history.

That's why IV rank is important. It tells you whether Implied Volatility is high or low at a particular point in time, depending on the actual volatility history of the stock.

IV Rank is between 0%-100%. If a stock's IV rank is closer to 0%, it means that the implied volatility is low, relative to the history of the stock. That means it might be a good time to buy a call or put.

If a stock's IV rank is closer to 100%, it means that the implied volatility is high, relative to the history of the stock. That means it might be a good time to sell a call or put, and receive the higher premiums.

## How to use IV Rank

### Buying call/put options
a. Choose a stock you want to buy options on
b. Choose a target price and expiration date. This is flexible and can change with time
c. Check IV rank. IV rank can be found at Market Chameleon (https://marketchameleon.com/Symbols/FindTicker)
d. Wait for IV rank to be 40% or lower. It is preferable to have IV rank below 20% to get the best deal.
e. Buy call/put options that you can afford.

### Selling call/put options
a. Choose a stock you want to sell options on
b. Choose a target price and expiration date. This is flexible and can change with time
c. Check IV rank. IV rank can be found at Market Chameleon (https://marketchameleon.com/Symbols/FindTicker)
d. Wait for IV rank to above 60% or lower. It is preferable to have IV rank below 80% to get the best deal.
e. Sell secured call/put options that you can afford.

# Examples

1. Let's look at RIO stock below. The important metric below is the IV rank. The IV rank is 42%. If you're looking to buy options, wait for it to get below 40%. The best deals are when the IV rank is below 20%.

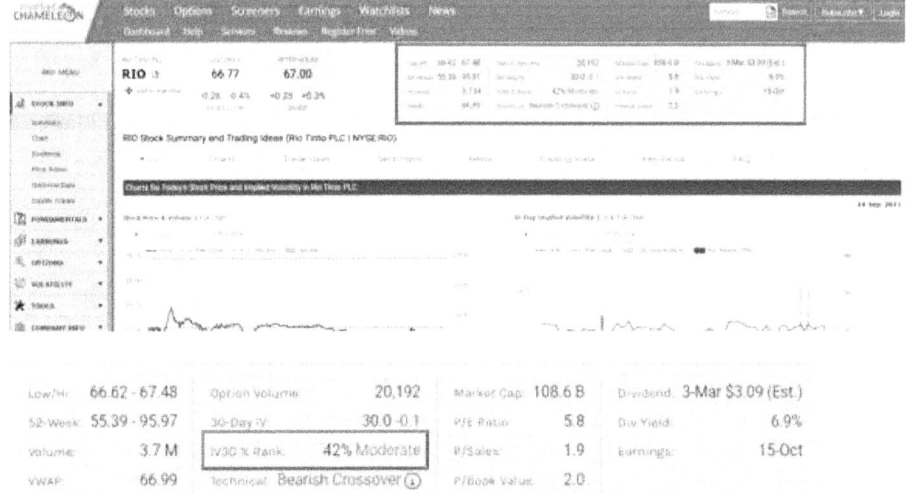

2. Let's look at Apple (AAPL) stock below. The important metric below is the IV rank. The IV rank is 10%. This is a good time to buy call/put options as the implied volatility is lowest; and options prices are lowest.

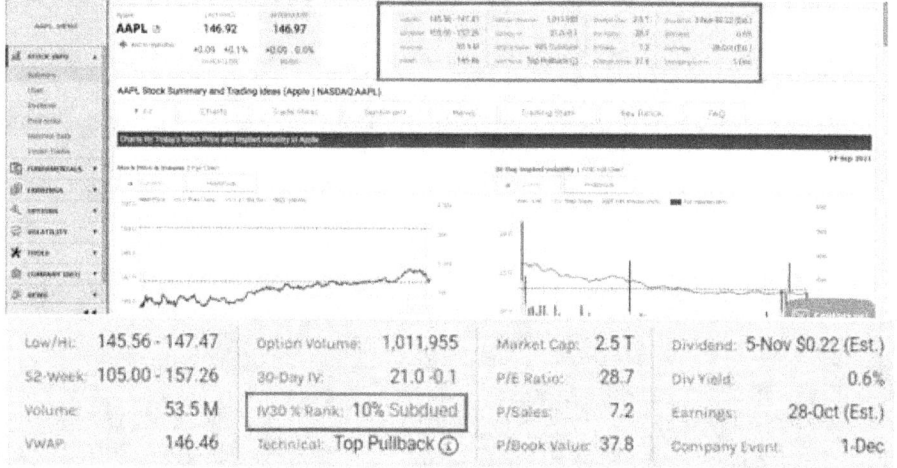

3. Let's look at NAT stock below. The important metric below is the IV rank. The IV rank is 86%. This is a good time to sell options, as you would get higher premiums.

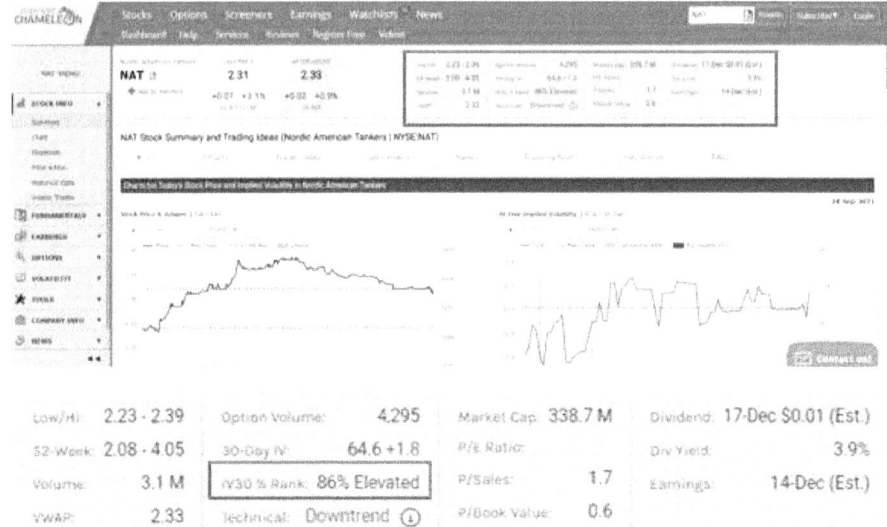

## Final Worksheet

This chapter is a test of what you've learned in this book so far.

It's also a great form of revision to ensure that you get the most out of this book.

1. What is the minimum number of shares you need to own to sell a call option?
    a. 200
    b. 10
    c. 100
    d. 34
2. When do you need to spend money on an option?
    a. Buying an option
    b. Selling an option
3. When do you receive money from an option in the form of a premium?
    a. Buying an option
    b. Selling an option
4. What kind of option means you have to buy 100 shares of a stock when it drops below a particular price within a certain period?
    a. Buying a call option
    b. Selling a call option
    c. Buying a put option
    d. Selling a put option
5. What kind of options lets you sell 100 shares of a stock when it goes over a particular price within a certain period?
    a. Buying a call option
    b. Selling a call option
    c. Buying a put option
    d. Selling a put option
6. Which is more significant when decided when to buy a call option?
    a. Volatility
    b. Implied Volatility
    c. IV Rank
7. If you're looking to sell a put option, what is the ideal IV rank for it?
    a. 65%
    b. 85%
    c. 15%
    d. 40%

8. If you're looking to buy a call option, what is the ideal IV rank for it?
    a. 65%
    b. 85%
    c. 15%
    d. 40%
9. If Apple stock has an IV rank of 60% and you're looking to sell an option, what should you do?
    a. Sell a call option now
    b. Wait till the IV rank hits 80%
    c. Wait till the IV rank hits 40%
    d. Wait till the IV rank hits 20%
10. If Samsung has an IV rank of 10%, and you're looking to buy a put option, what should you do?
    a. Buy the put option now
    b. Wait till the IV rank hits 80%
    c. Wait till the IV rank hits 50%
    d. Wait till the IV rank hits 70%
11. Which trading strategy is the best to use if you expect the stock to stay within a fixed range?
    a. Call Option
    b. Shorting a Stock
    c. Put Option
    d. Iron Condor
    e. Collar
12. Which trading strategy is the best to use if you expect the stock to crash?
    a. Call Option
    b. Shorting a Stock
    c. Put Option
    d. Iron Condor
    e. Collar
13. Which options strategy helps to reduce the cost of a put option?
    a. Call Option
    b. Shorting a Stock
    c. Put Option
    d. Iron Condor

e. Collar
14. Which options strategy is an alternative to buying a stock, which allows for less risk and more scale?
    a. Call Option
    b. Shorting a Stock
    c. Put Option
    d. Iron Condor
    e. Collar
15. Which is the most dangerous strategy in the stock market?
    a. Call Option
    b. Shorting a Stock
    c. Put Option
    d. Iron Condor
    e. Collar

16. Jo buys 1 iron condor for Southern Copper stock that expires in 50 days. The two puts are at $40 and $45; and the two calls are at $70 and $75. Estimate the net premium received and draw a chart of price at expiration vs profit for the options contract.

**Setup (Short Iron Condor — net credit):**
- Sell 1 put @ strike $45
- Buy 1 put @ strike $40
- Sell 1 call @ strike $70
- Buy 1 call @ strike $75

**Premiums from the option chain (SCCO, 50 DTE, last trade $56.14):**

| Option | Bid | Ask | Mid |
|---|---|---|---|
| 40 Put | 0.05 | 0.25 | 0.15 |
| 45 Put | 0.35 | 0.50 | 0.425 |
| 70 Call | 0.15 | 0.25 | 0.20 |
| 75 Call | 0.00 | 0.15 | 0.075 |

**Net premium received (using mid prices):**

$$\text{Net credit} = (0.425 - 0.15) + (0.20 - 0.075) = 0.275 + 0.125 = 0.40$$

Per contract (×100 shares): **≈ $40 net premium received**.

**Key levels at expiration:**
- Max profit = net premium = **+$40** (when $45 \le S_T \le 70$)
- Max loss = (width of wing − premium) × 100 = $(5 - 0.40) \times 100 = -\$460$ (when $S_T \le 40$ or $S_T \ge 75$)
- Breakevens: $45 - 0.40 = \$44.60$ (lower) and $70 + 0.40 = \$70.40$ (upper)

**Profit vs. Price at Expiration Chart:**

```
Profit ($)
  +40 |           _____
      |          /                        \
    0 |---------/--------------------------\---------  S_T
      |        /|                          |\
      |       / |                          | \
      |      /  |                          |  \
 -460 |_____/___|_____|_____
           40  44.60                     70.40 75
                45                        70
```

- Flat at −$460 for $S_T \le 40$
- Rises linearly from −$460 at $S_T = 40$ to +$40 at $S_T = 45$ (breakeven at $44.60)
- Flat at +$40 for $45 \le S_T \le 70$
- Falls linearly from +$40 at $S_T = 70$ to −$460 at $S_T = 75$ (breakeven at $70.40)
- Flat at −$460 for $S_T \ge 75$

## 17. Iron Condor on 3D Systems (DDD) — 15 days to expiration

**Stock:** DDD @ $27.57 (Oct 15, 2021 expiration, 15 days)

A long iron condor is constructed by selling the inner options and buying the outer options:

| Leg | Action | Strike | Bid | Ask | Mid |
|---|---|---|---|---|---|
| Put  | Buy  | 20 | 0.00 | 0.05 | 0.025 |
| Put  | Sell | 22 | 0.05 | 0.15 | 0.100 |
| Call | Sell | 32 | 0.25 | 0.30 | 0.275 |
| Call | Buy  | 34 | 0.10 | 0.15 | 0.125 |

### Net Premium Received

$$\text{Net credit} = (0.100 + 0.275) - (0.025 + 0.125) = 0.225 \text{ per share}$$

Per contract (×100 shares): **Net premium received ≈ $22.50**

### Profit at Expiration

- Width of each wing: $20 \to 22$ and $32 \to 34$ = $2.00
- **Max profit** = net credit = $0.225/share = **$22.50** (when $22 \le S_T \le 32$)
- **Max loss** = width − credit = $2.00 − 0.225 = $1.775/share = **−$177.50** (when $S_T \le 20$ or $S_T \ge 34$)
- Lower breakeven: $22 - 0.225 = 21.775$
- Upper breakeven: $32 + 0.225 = 32.225$

### Profit vs. Price at Expiration

```
Profit ($)
  +22.50 ┤            _____
         │           /              \
       0 ┤──────────/────────────────\──────────  S_T
         │         /21.78       32.22 \
         │        /                    \
 -177.50 ┤_____/                      _____
         └──┬────┬──────────────────┬────┬────── 
           20   22                 32   34
```

- $S_T \le 20$: Profit = −$177.50
- $20 \le S_T \le 22$: rises linearly from −$177.50 to +$22.50
- $22 \le S_T \le 32$: Profit = +$22.50
- $32 \le S_T \le 34$: falls linearly from +$22.50 to −$177.50
- $S_T \ge 34$: Profit = −$177.50

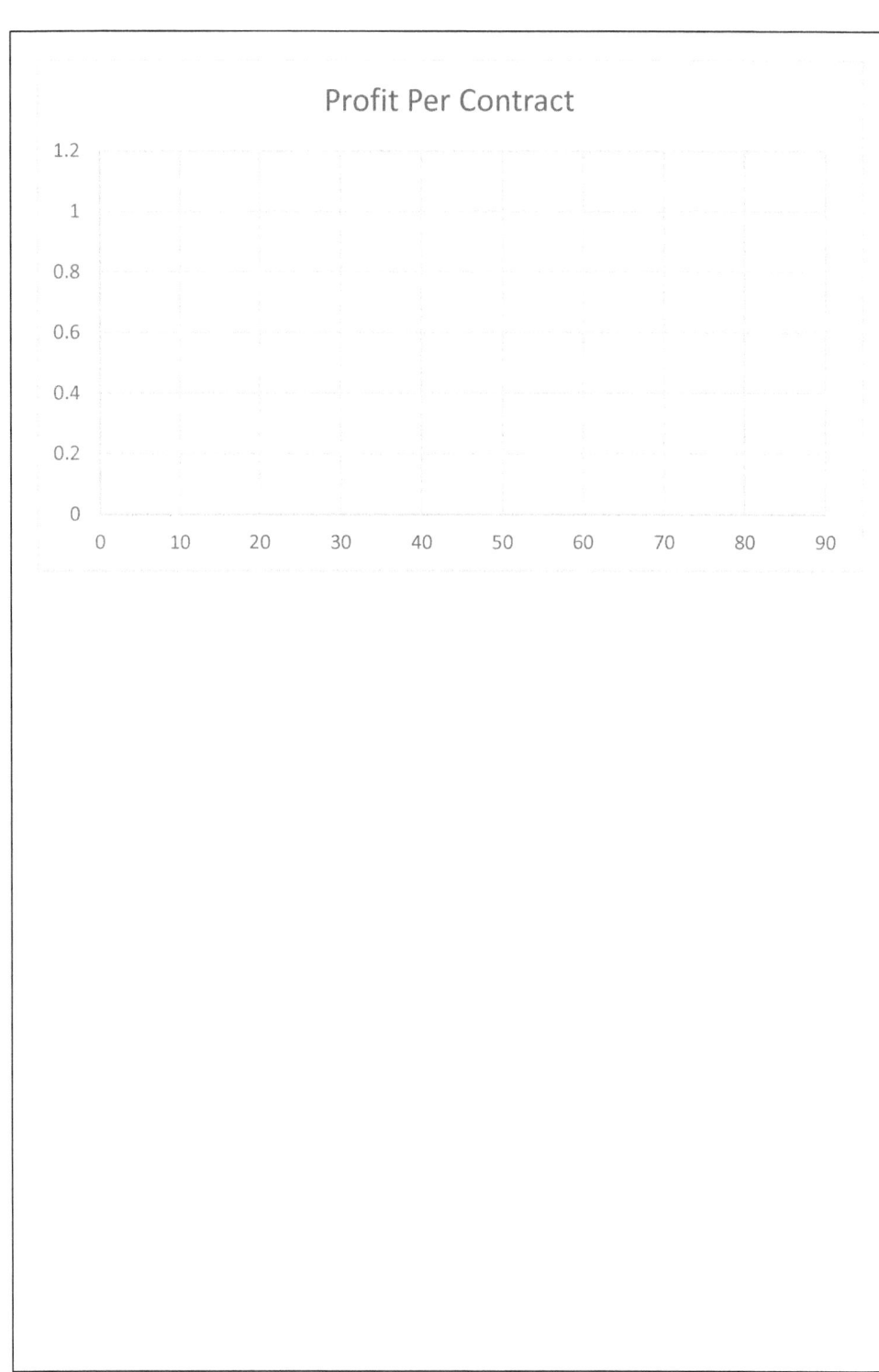

18. Bob sells 1 put option for Northern Star stock that expires in 141 days. The strike price is at $12.50. Estimate the net premium received and draw a chart of price at expiration vs profit for the options contract.

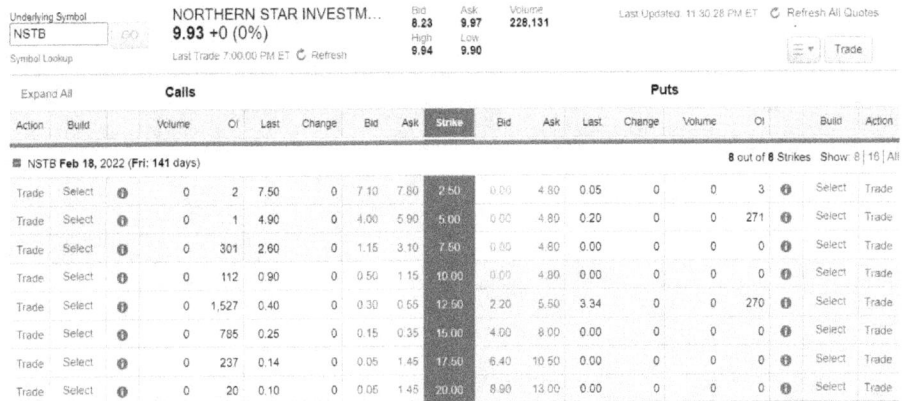

| Action | Build | | Volume | OI | Last | Change | Bid | Ask | Strike | Bid | Ask | Last | Change | Volume | OI | | Build | Action |
|---|---|---|---|---|---|---|---|---|---|---|---|---|---|---|---|---|---|---|
| NSTB Feb 18, 2022 (Fri: 141 days) | | | | | | | | | | | | | | | | | 8 out of 8 Strikes Show: 8 \| 16 \| All | |
| Trade | Select | | 0 | 2 | 7.50 | 0 | 7.10 | 7.80 | 2.50 | 0.00 | 4.80 | 0.05 | 0 | 0 | 3 | | Select | Trade |
| Trade | Select | | 0 | 1 | 4.90 | 0 | 4.00 | 5.90 | 5.00 | 0.00 | 4.80 | 0.20 | 0 | 0 | 271 | | Select | Trade |
| Trade | Select | | 0 | 301 | 2.60 | 0 | 1.15 | 3.10 | 7.50 | 0.00 | 4.80 | 0.00 | 0 | 0 | 0 | | Select | Trade |
| Trade | Select | | 0 | 112 | 0.90 | 0 | 0.50 | 1.15 | 10.00 | 0.00 | 4.80 | 0.00 | 0 | 0 | 0 | | Select | Trade |
| Trade | Select | | 0 | 1,527 | 0.40 | 0 | 0.30 | 0.55 | 12.50 | 2.20 | 5.50 | 3.34 | 0 | 0 | 270 | | Select | Trade |
| Trade | Select | | 0 | 785 | 0.25 | 0 | 0.15 | 0.35 | 15.00 | 4.00 | 8.00 | 0.00 | 0 | 0 | 0 | | Select | Trade |
| Trade | Select | | 0 | 237 | 0.14 | 0 | 0.05 | 1.45 | 17.50 | 6.40 | 10.50 | 0.00 | 0 | 0 | 0 | | Select | Trade |
| Trade | Select | | 0 | 20 | 0.10 | 0 | 0.05 | 1.45 | 20.00 | 8.90 | 13.00 | 0.00 | 0 | 0 | 0 | | Select | Trade |

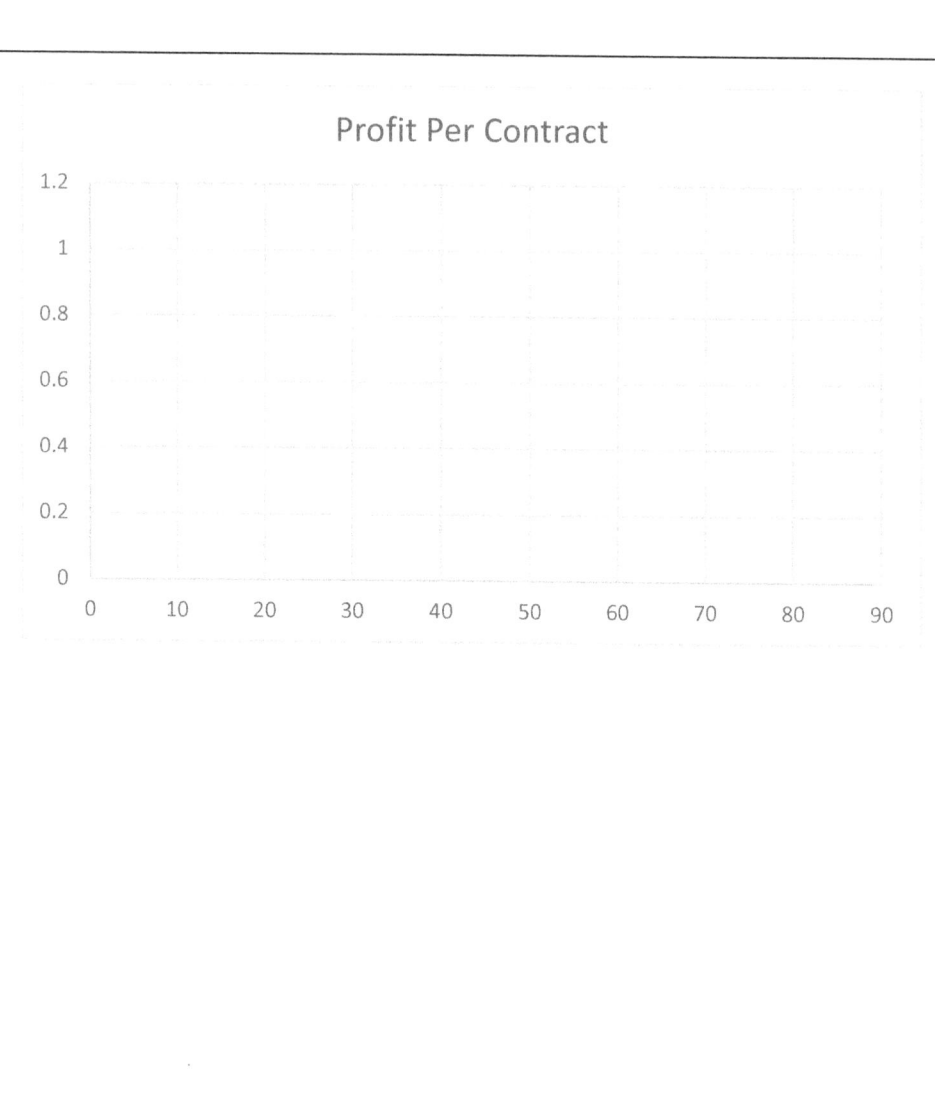

19. Toby buys 1 call option for GLD stock that expires in 260 days. The strike price is at $170. Estimate the cost of the option and draw a chart of price at expiration vs profit for the options contract.

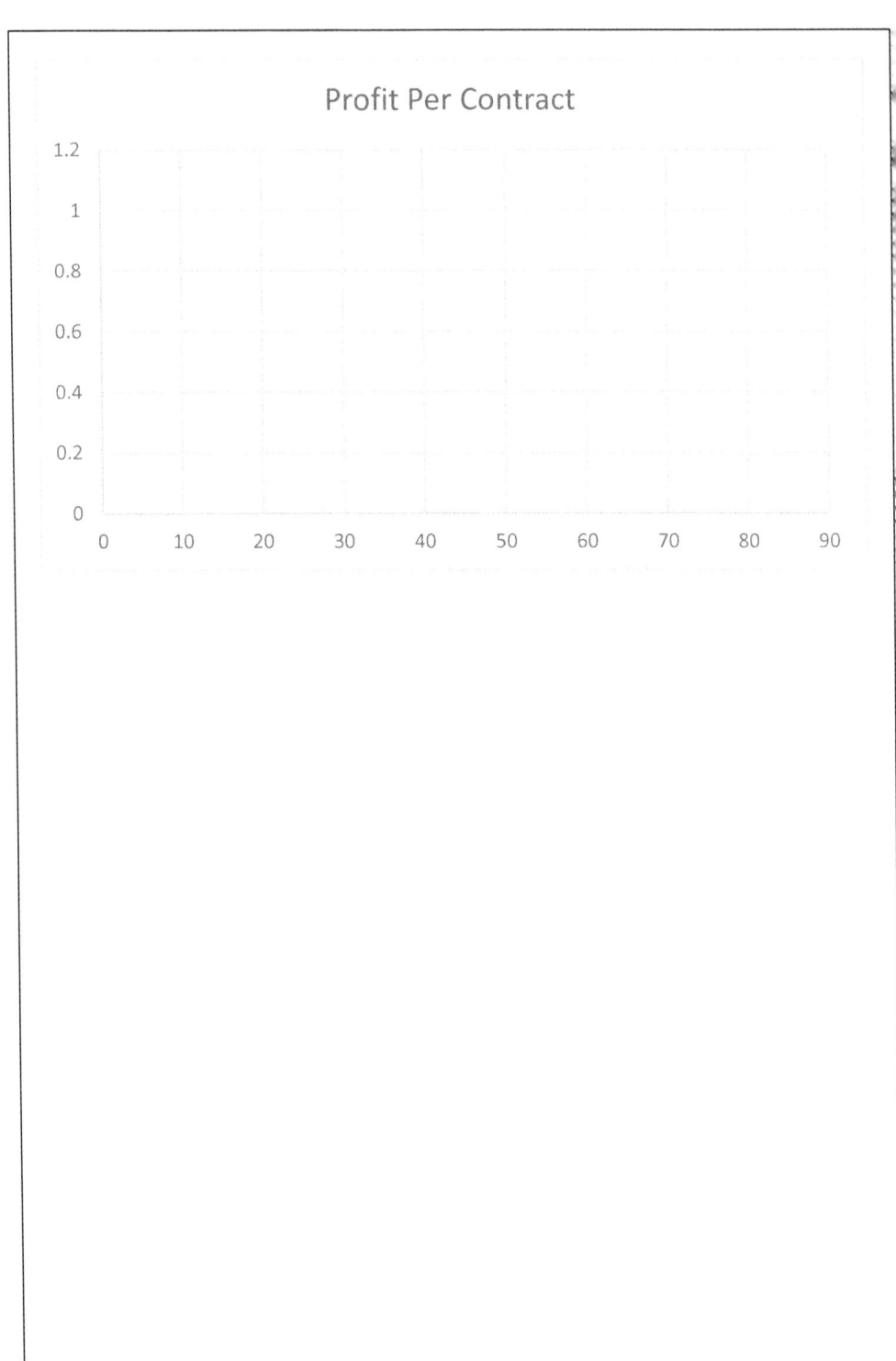

20. Sam buys 1 put option for Ford stock that expires in 169 days. The strike price is at $12. Estimate the cost of the option and draw a chart of price at expiration vs profit for the options contract.

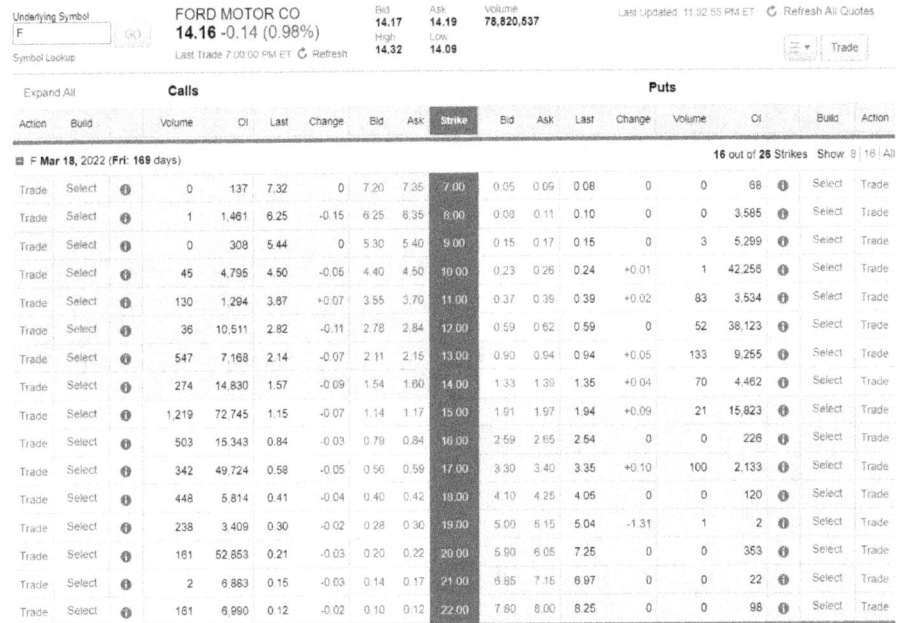

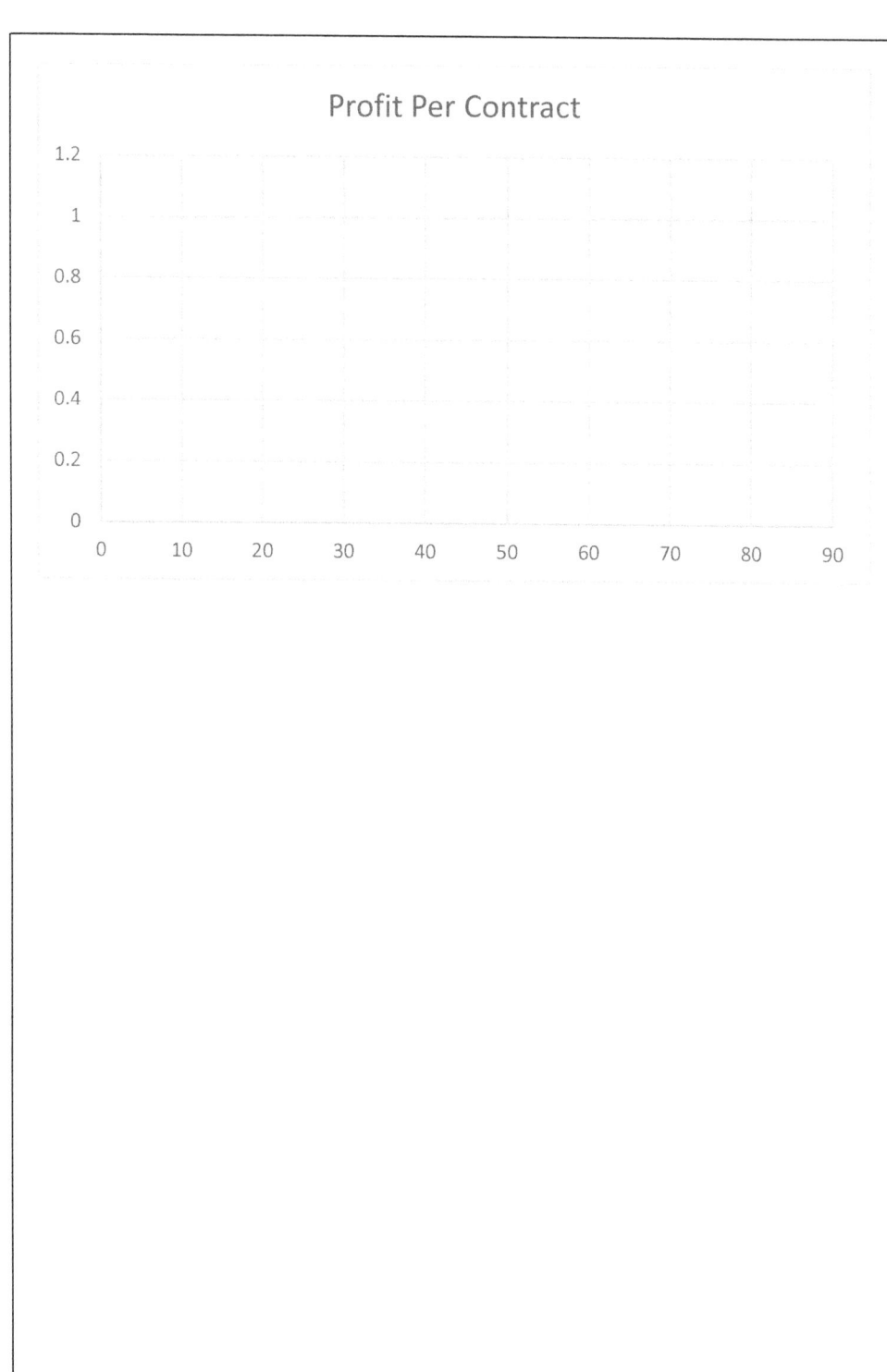

21. Tim buys 1 put option for Ford stock that expires in 196 days. The strike price is at $50. He then sells 1 call at $65 to offset the cost of the put.

    Estimate the cost of the option and draw a chart of price at expiration vs profit for the options contract.

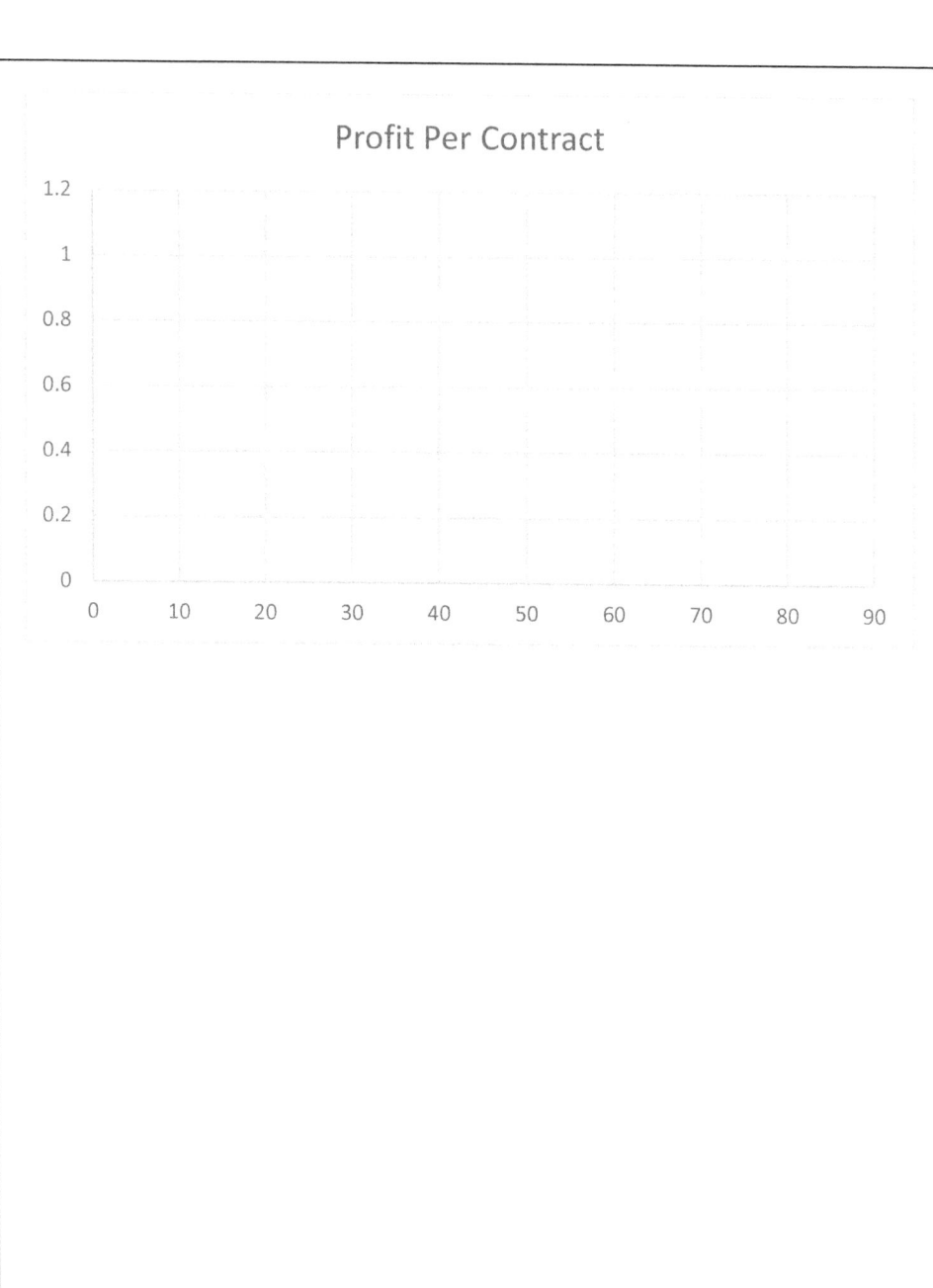

22. Kandy buys 1 put option for Ark investment stock that expires in 113 days. The strike price is at $100. He then sells 1 call at $110 to offset the cost of the put.
Estimate the cost of the option and draw a chart of price at expiration vs profit for the options contract.

**Underlying Symbol:** ARKK
**ARK INNOVATION ETF** 110.53 +0.81 (0.74%)
Bid 110.84  Ask 110.96  Volume 8,556,135
High 111.71  Low 110.00
Last Trade 8:00:00 PM ET
Last Updated: 11:49:16 PM ET

**ARKK Jan 21, 2022 (Fri: 113 days)**
16 out of 86 Strikes

| | | Calls | | | | | | | | Puts | | | | | | |
|---|---|---|---|---|---|---|---|---|---|---|---|---|---|---|---|---|
| Action | Build | Volume | OI | Last | Change | Bid | Ask | Strike | Bid | Ask | Last | Change | Volume | OI | Build | Action |
| Trade | Select | 0 | 58 | 30.00 | 0 | 17.15 | 17.55 | 96.96 | 4.75 | 5.00 | 4.33 | 0 | 0 | 701 | Select | Trade |
| Trade | Select | 0 | 1,334 | 16.55 | 0 | 15.40 | 15.75 | 97.96 | 5.00 | 5.25 | 5.15 | 0 | 0 | 1,094 | Select | Trade |
| Trade | Select | 0 | 197 | 17.25 | 0 | 15.65 | 16.00 | 98.96 | 5.30 | 5.50 | 5.33 | -0.02 | 1 | 974 | Select | Trade |
| Trade | Select | 57 | 2,563 | 15.77 | +1.35 | 14.85 | 15.25 | 100.00 | 5.70 | 5.85 | 5.60 | -0.30 | 2,382 | 24,557 | Select | Trade |
| Trade | Select | 0 | 1,900 | 19.22 | 0 | 12.90 | 13.25 | 102.96 | 6.55 | 6.80 | 6.48 | -0.33 | 24 | 2,215 | Select | Trade |
| Trade | Select | 45 | 1,456 | 12.22 | +0.97 | 11.55 | 11.90 | 105.00 | 6.95 | 7.55 | 7.30 | -0.15 | 1,929 | 10,039 | Select | Trade |
| Trade | Select | 14 | 2,071 | 9.86 | +0.26 | 9.75 | 10.10 | 107.96 | 8.45 | 8.85 | 8.40 | 0 | 6 | 2,677 | Select | Trade |
| Trade | Select | 63 | 3,389 | 8.75 | +0.45 | 8.65 | 8.95 | 110.00 | 9.40 | 9.60 | 9.58 | -0.04 | 105 | 15,447 | Select | Trade |
| Trade | Select | 3 | 559 | 7.15 | -0.10 | 7.15 | 7.45 | 112.96 | 10.80 | 11.15 | 10.65 | -0.79 | 6 | 5,289 | Select | Trade |
| Trade | Select | 52 | 6,517 | 6.30 | +0.35 | 6.15 | 6.50 | 115.00 | 11.90 | 12.25 | 11.66 | -0.34 | 35 | 4,403 | Select | Trade |
| Trade | Select | 12 | 1,012 | 5.29 | +0.26 | 4.95 | 5.30 | 117.96 | 13.65 | 14.05 | 13.60 | -0.65 | 1 | 764 | Select | Trade |
| Trade | Select | 95 | 7,498 | 4.55 | +0.42 | 4.20 | 4.50 | 120.00 | 14.90 | 15.40 | 15.15 | -0.50 | 98 | 11,773 | Select | Trade |
| Trade | Select | 7 | 1,413 | 3.30 | -0.13 | 3.30 | 3.55 | 122.96 | 16.90 | 17.50 | 13.05 | 0 | 0 | 3,682 | Select | Trade |
| Trade | Select | 31 | 5,255 | 2.86 | -0.08 | 2.76 | 2.98 | 125.00 | 18.45 | 18.95 | 18.15 | -1.05 | 4 | 5,534 | Select | Trade |
| Trade | Select | 1 | 946 | 2.21 | -0.09 | 2.11 | 2.33 | 127.96 | 20.70 | 21.30 | 21.84 | 0 | 0 | 777 | Select | Trade |
| Trade | Select | 45 | 3,629 | 1.94 | +0.11 | 1.75 | 1.96 | 130.00 | 22.40 | 23.05 | 22.70 | -0.15 | 3 | 6,839 | Select | Trade |

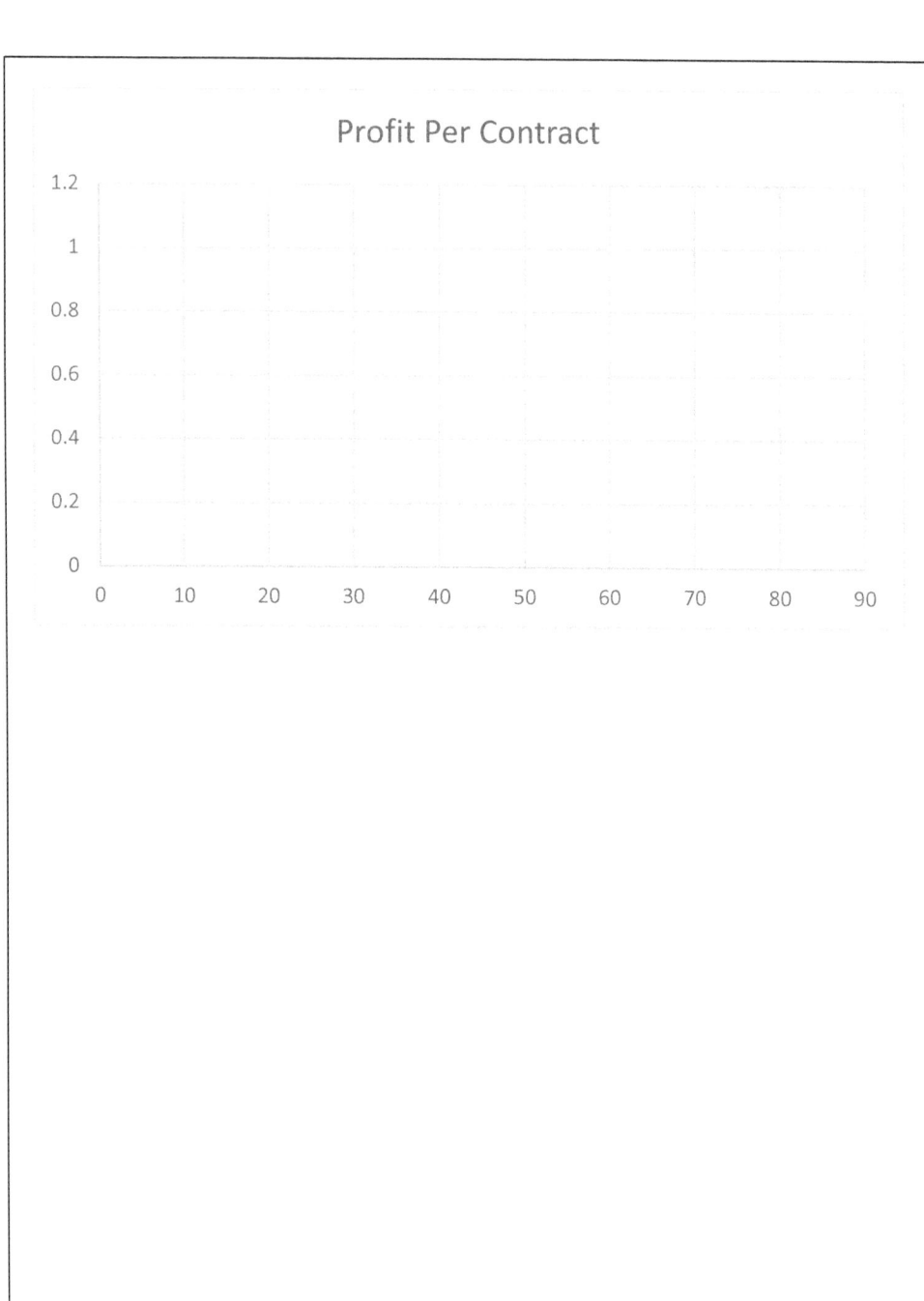

23. Sammy buys a collar for EDU stock; with the put price at $1.5 and the call at $2.

Estimate the cost of the option and draw a chart of price at expiration vs profit for the options contract.

24. Elona buys a put option for Tesla stock; with the strike price at $750. Estimate the cost of the option and draw a chart of price at expiration vs profit for the options contract.

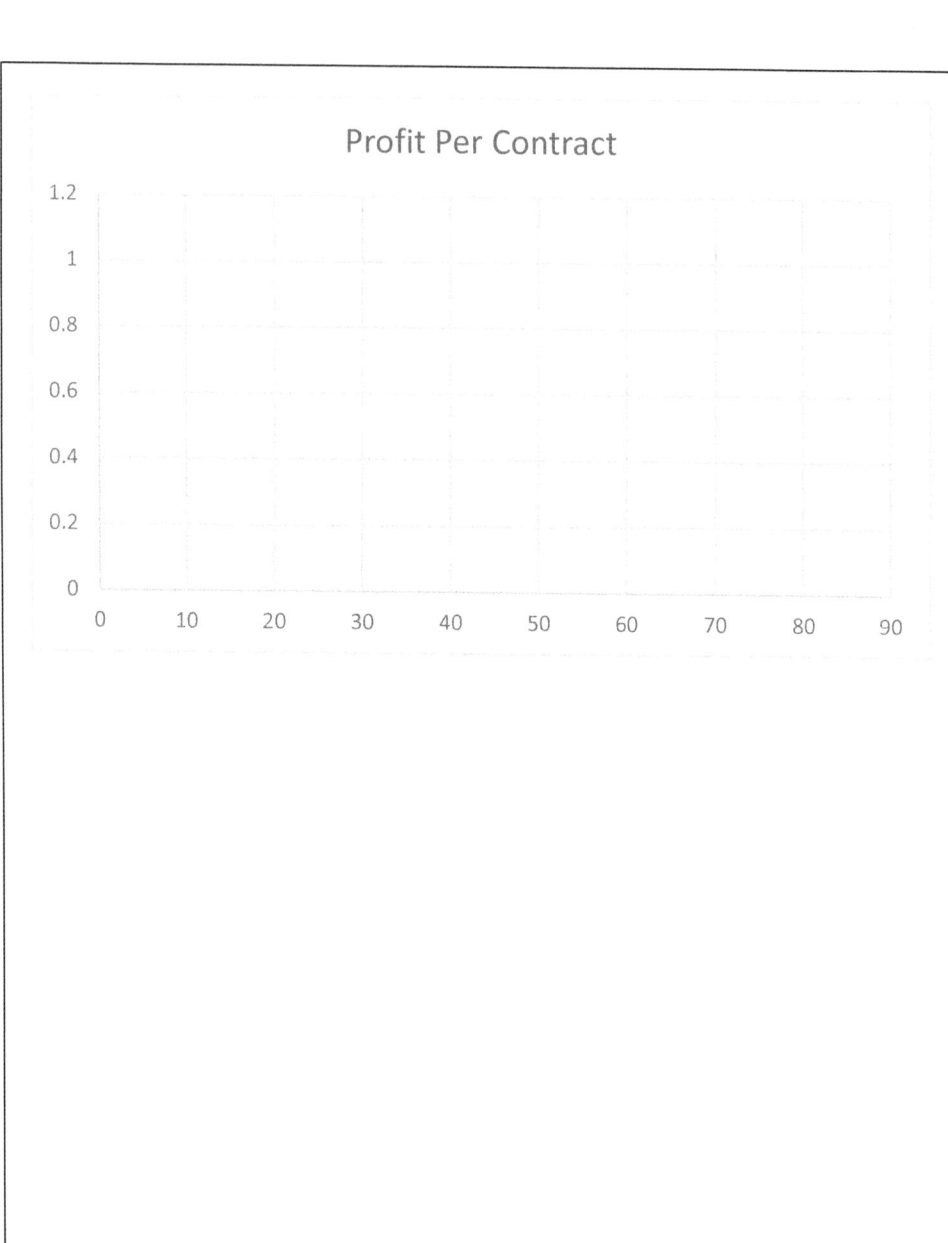

25. Fiona buys a put option for Microsoft stock; with the strike price at $250.

Estimate the cost of the option and draw a chart of price at expiration vs profit for the options contract.

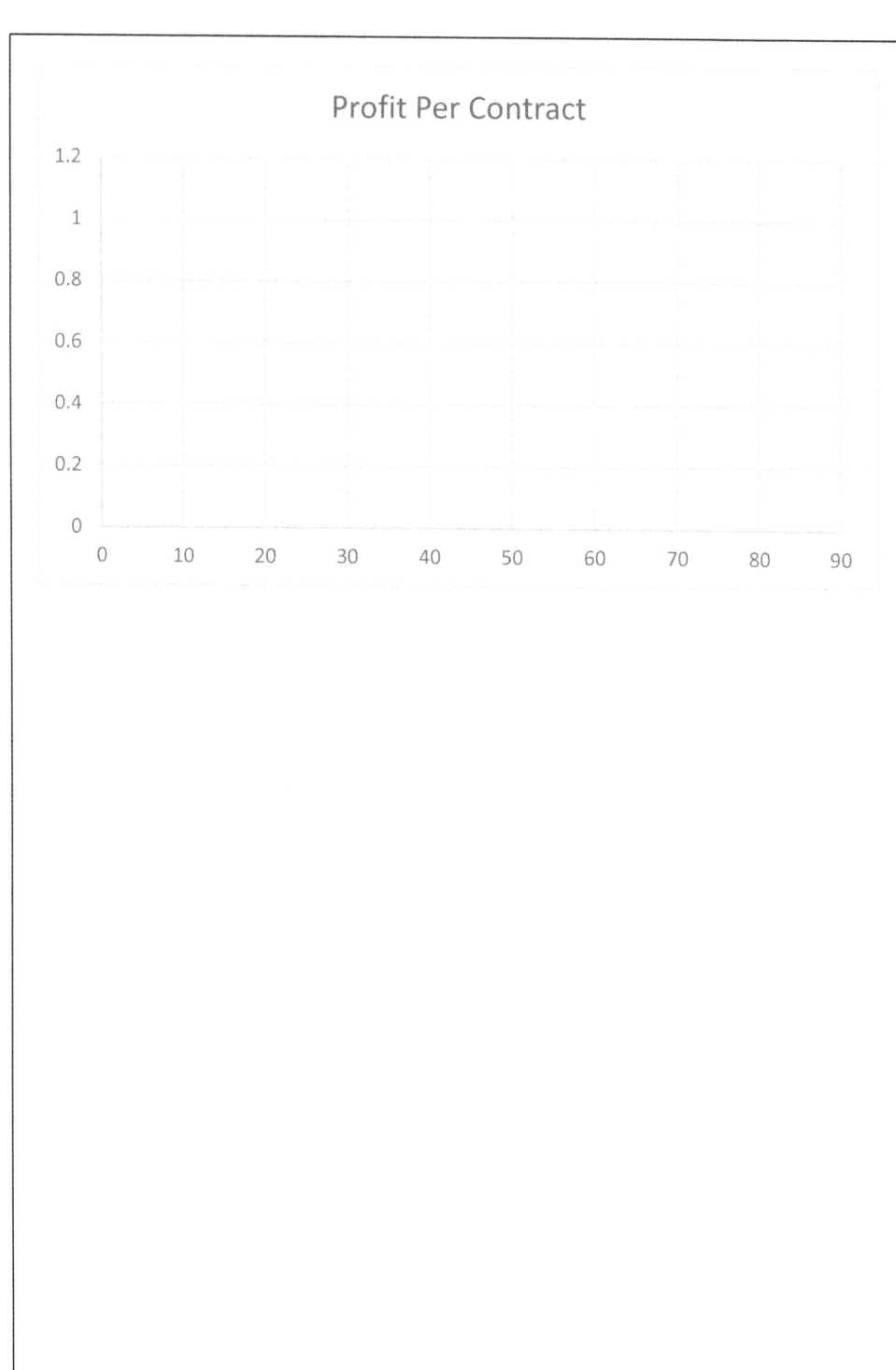

26. Bob purchases an iron condor for Advanced Micro Devices (AMD) that expires in 77 days.

The put strike prices are $85 and $90; while the call strike prices are $135 and $140.

   a. What is the net premium he receives?
   b. What happens if AMD expires at $150?
   c. What happens if AMD expires at $125?
   d. What happens if AMD expires at $80?
   e. What happens if AMD expires at $136?

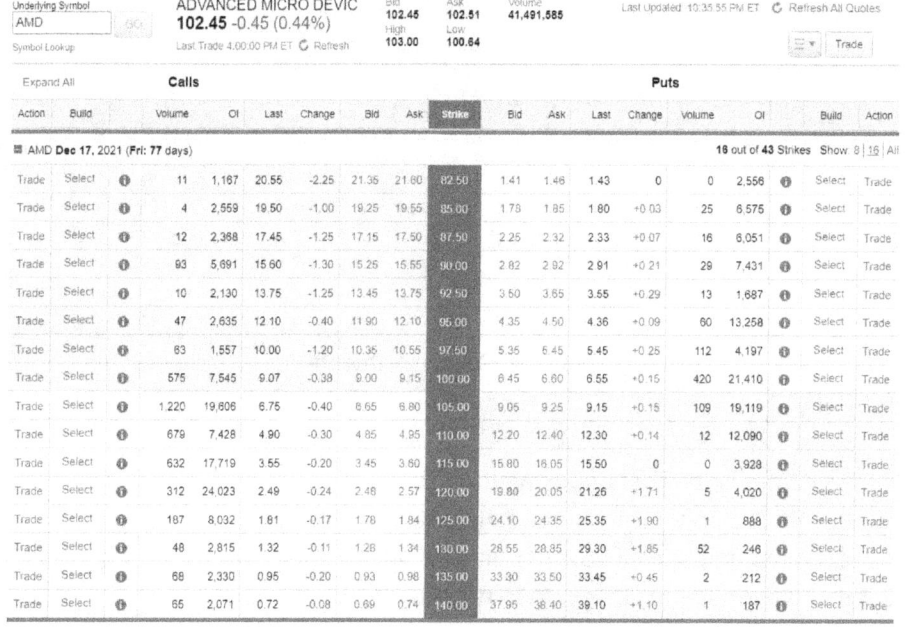

27. William owns 200 shares of Toyota Motors. He sells a collar; buying a put at $160 and selling a call at $165. It expires in 112 days.

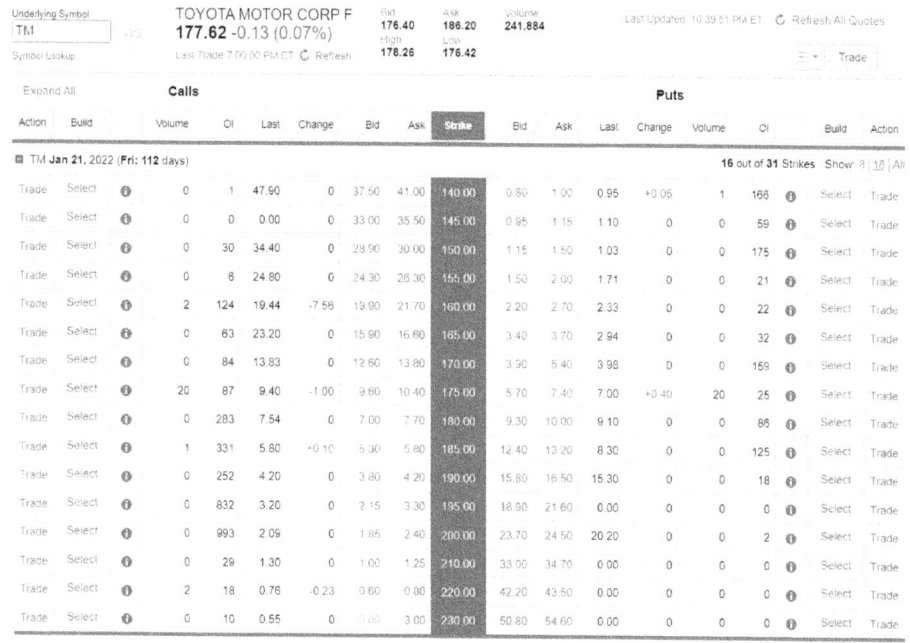

Source: Charles Schwab

a. What is the cost of buying the collar?
b. What happens if Toyota is at $150 at expiration?
c. What happens if Toyota is at $200 at expiration?
d. What happens if Toyota is at $170 at expiration?

Assume that the minimum prices are paid for buying/selling puts/calls

28. Tim owns 100 shares of Intel stock, and he wants to complete a vertical spread where he sells a call option at $40 and buy a call option at $45.

  i. How many contracts can he sell?
  ii. What is the net premium that he receives?
  iii. What happens if Intel stock is at $70 at expiration?
  iv. What happens if Intel stock is at $30 at expiration?

Underlying Symbol: INTC
INTEL CORP  53.86 +0.58 (1.09%)
Last Trade 4:00:01 PM ET
Bid 53.83  Ask 53.93  Volume 19,895,101
High 54.105  Low 53.05
Last Updated 10:41:58 PM ET

INTC Oct 01, 2021 (Expires today)

| | | | Calls | | | | | | Strike | | | Puts | | | | | | |
|---|---|---|---|---|---|---|---|---|---|---|---|---|---|---|---|---|---|---|
| Action | Build | | Volume | OI | Last | Change | Bid | Ask | Strike | Bid | Ask | Last | Change | Volume | OI | | Build | Action |
| Trade | Select | | 168 | 184 | 3.90 | +0.23 | 3.75 | 3.95 | 50.00 | 0.00 | 0.01 | 0.01 | | 0 | 15 | 2,623 | Select | Trade |
| Trade | Select | | 1 | 24 | 2.60 | -1.45 | 3.25 | 3.45 | 50.50 | 0.00 | 0.01 | 0.01 | | 0 | 0 | 347 | Select | Trade |
| Trade | Select | | 16 | 27 | 3.00 | +0.35 | 2.71 | 2.94 | 51.00 | 0.00 | 0.01 | 0.01 | -0.01 | 9 | 1,295 | | Select | Trade |
| Trade | Select | | 1 | 13 | 1.61 | -0.33 | 2.24 | 2.67 | 51.50 | 0.06 | 0.01 | 0.01 | | 0 | 44 | 2,421 | Select | Trade |
| Trade | Select | | 104 | 621 | 1.93 | +0.26 | 1.75 | 2.12 | 52.00 | 0.00 | 0.01 | 0.01 | -0.03 | 381 | 1,610 | | Select | Trade |
| Trade | Select | | 464 | 483 | 1.40 | +0.14 | 1.24 | 1.48 | 52.50 | 0.00 | 0.01 | 0.01 | -0.10 | 511 | 1,866 | | Select | Trade |
| Trade | Select | | 426 | 867 | 0.83 | +0.25 | 0.76 | 0.98 | 53.00 | 0.00 | 0.01 | 0.01 | -0.19 | 1,790 | 5,419 | | Select | Trade |
| Trade | Select | | 5,425 | 1,164 | 0.40 | +0.14 | 0.28 | 0.43 | 53.50 | 0.00 | 0.01 | 0.02 | -0.40 | 3,714 | 2,109 | | Select | Trade |
| Trade | Select | | 3,981 | 3,958 | 0.01 | -0.09 | 0.00 | 0.01 | 54.00 | 0.08 | 0.26 | 0.16 | -0.64 | 12,848 | 9,958 | | Select | Trade |
| Trade | Select | | 782 | 4,076 | 0.01 | -0.02 | 0.00 | 0.01 | 54.50 | 0.55 | 0.74 | 0.61 | -0.19 | 398 | 2,115 | | Select | Trade |
| Trade | Select | | 845 | 6,733 | 0.01 | -0.01 | 0.00 | 0.01 | 55.00 | 1.06 | 1.26 | 1.16 | -0.26 | 896 | 1,654 | | Select | Trade |
| Trade | Select | | 713 | 2,749 | 0.01 | 0 | 0.00 | 0.01 | 55.50 | 1.47 | 1.76 | 1.67 | -0.30 | 197 | 263 | | Select | Trade |
| Trade | Select | | 213 | 8,957 | 0.01 | 0 | 0.00 | 0.01 | 56.00 | 2.07 | 2.33 | 2.00 | -0.57 | 259 | 481 | | Select | Trade |
| Trade | Select | | 32 | 863 | 0.01 | -0.01 | 0.00 | 0.01 | 56.50 | 2.55 | 2.78 | 2.68 | -0.30 | 144 | 333 | | Select | Trade |
| Trade | Select | | 26 | 5,598 | 0.01 | 0 | 0.00 | 0.01 | 57.00 | 3.05 | 3.25 | 2.98 | -0.44 | 36 | 277 | | Select | Trade |
| Trade | Select | | 0 | 513 | 0.01 | 0 | 0.00 | 0.01 | 57.50 | 3.55 | 3.75 | 3.30 | 0 | 0 | 0 | | Select | Trade |

16 out of 40 Strikes  Show: 8 | 16 | All

Source: Charles Schwab

29. You sell 1 put option of Electronic Arts below.

| | | Calls | | | | | | Strike | | | Puts | | | | | | |
|---|---|---|---|---|---|---|---|---|---|---|---|---|---|---|---|---|---|
| Action | Build | Volume | OI | Last | Change | Bid | Ask | Strike | Bid | Ask | Last | Change | Volume | OI | Build | Action |
| Trade | Select | 0 | 43 | 35.05 | 0 | 38.45 | 41.85 | 105.00 | 1.08 | 1.23 | 1.30 | 0 | 0 | 1,584 | Select | Trade |
| Trade | Select | 0 | 157 | 34.95 | 0 | 33.90 | 37.15 | 110.00 | 1.44 | 1.55 | 1.53 | -0.09 | 2 | 4,975 | Select | Trade |
| Trade | Select | 0 | 235 | 16.20 | 0 | 30.10 | 31.45 | 115.00 | 1.81 | 1.99 | 1.95 | -0.09 | 1 | 1,173 | Select | Trade |
| Trade | Select | 1 | 697 | 25.50 | -0.50 | 25.75 | 26.45 | 120.00 | 2.40 | 2.59 | 2.48 | -0.60 | 19 | 3,294 | Select | Trade |
| Trade | Select | 0 | 764 | 21.23 | 0 | 21.80 | 22.45 | 125.00 | 3.25 | 3.45 | 4.07 | -0.18 | 5 | 1,488 | Select | Trade |
| Trade | Select | 10 | 743 | 18.35 | +0.60 | 17.90 | 18.35 | 130.00 | 4.30 | 4.60 | 4.55 | 0 | 0 | 2,524 | Select | Trade |
| Trade | Select | 2 | 3,227 | 14.65 | +0.05 | 14.25 | 14.75 | 135.00 | 5.70 | 6.00 | 6.65 | +0.47 | 4 | 1,005 | Select | Trade |
| Trade | Select | 7 | 1,691 | 11.55 | +0.86 | 11.25 | 11.65 | 140.00 | 7.50 | 7.35 | 7.68 | -0.39 | 11 | 931 | Select | Trade |
| Trade | Select | 22 | 1,782 | 8.84 | -0.11 | 8.55 | 8.90 | 145.00 | 9.85 | 10.20 | 15.25 | 0 | 0 | 578 | Select | Trade |
| Trade | Select | 7 | 2,261 | 6.35 | +0.15 | 6.35 | 6.75 | 150.00 | 12.70 | 13.25 | 14.50 | 0 | 0 | 558 | Select | Trade |
| Trade | Select | 4 | 1,040 | 4.76 | +0.01 | 4.70 | 5.00 | 155.00 | 16.00 | 16.45 | 18.70 | -1.25 | 2 | 73 | Select | Trade |
| Trade | Select | 3 | 745 | 3.35 | -0.48 | 3.40 | 3.65 | 160.00 | 19.85 | 20.10 | 21.90 | +1.70 | 25 | 51 | Select | Trade |
| Trade | Select | 0 | 270 | 2.83 | 0 | 2.45 | 2.73 | 165.00 | 23.40 | 25.20 | 37.00 | 0 | 0 | 41 | Select | Trade |
| Trade | Select | 9 | 3,256 | 1.81 | -0.25 | 1.80 | 2.03 | 170.00 | 26.15 | 28.40 | 30.75 | 0 | 0 | 11 | Select | Trade |
| Trade | Select | 0 | 356 | 0.95 | 0 | 1.26 | 1.42 | 175.00 | 32.15 | 34.05 | 31.63 | 0 | 0 | 7 | Select | Trade |
| Trade | Select | 0 | 455 | 0.50 | 0 | 0.93 | 1.13 | 180.00 | 35.55 | 38.95 | 45.15 | 0 | 0 | 8 | Select | Trade |

EA Jan 21, 2022 (Fri: 112 days)

- When's the expiration date of the options above?
- What is the premium you would receive for selling 1 put option at a strike price of $120? Assume that you get paid the minimum amount in the range.
- How much cash do you need as collateral to sell 1 put option at a strike price of $120?
- What happens if EA stock is at $160 after 112 days?
- What happens if EA stock is at $90 after 112 days?

30. Jack buys 2 contracts of Twitter call options that expire in 168 days. The strike price for the contract is **$65**. Assume that Jack pays the minimum required premium for the stock.

If the Twitter price in 168 days is $100:

- How many shares of stock does Twitter have the option to buy?
- How much premium does Twitter pay for the contract? (Assume that Alice pays the minimum amount)
- How much profit does Twitter make in 168 days?

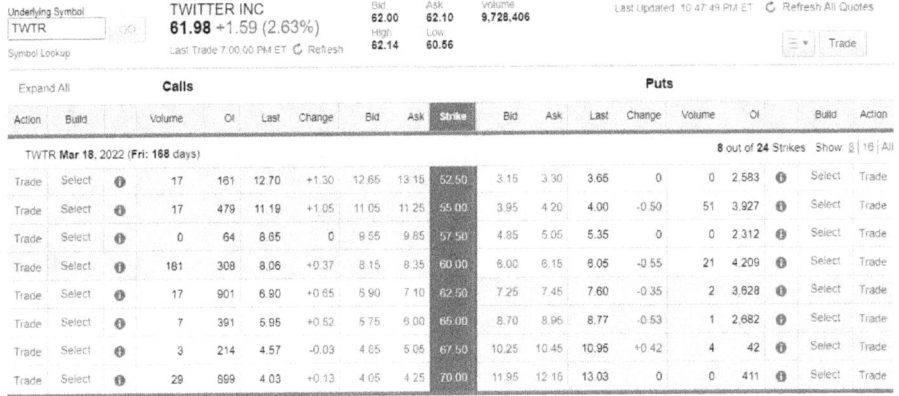

# Final Worksheet – Answers

1. What is the minimum number of shares you need to own to sell a call option?
    a. 200
    b. 10
    c. 100
    d. 34
2. When do you need to spend money on an option?
    a. Buying an option
    b. Selling an option
3. When do you receive money from an option in the form of a premium?
    a. Buying an option
    b. Selling an option
4. What kind of option means you have to buy 100 shares of a stock when it drops below a particular price within a certain period?
    a. Buying a call option
    b. Selling a call option
    c. Buying a put option
    d. Selling a put option
5. What kind of options lets you sell 100 shares of a stock when it goes over a particular price within a certain period?
    a. Buying a call option
    b. Selling a call option
    c. Buying a put option
    d. Selling a put option
6. Which is more significant when decided when to buy a call option?
    a. Volatility
    b. Implied Volatility
    c. IV Rank
7. If you're looking to sell a put option, what is the ideal IV rank for it?
    a. 65%
    b. 85%
    c. 15%
    d. 40%

8. If you're looking to buy a call option, what is the ideal IV rank for it?
    a. 65%
    b. 85%
    c. 15%
    d. 40%
9. If Apple stock has an IV rank of 60% and you're looking to sell an option, what should you do?
    a. Sell a call option now
    b. Not a bad time to sell, but better to wait till the IV rank hits 80%
    c. Not a bad time to sell, but better to wait till the IV rank hits 40%
    d. Not a bad time to sell, but better to wait till the IV rank hits 20%
10. If Samsung has an IV rank of 10%, and you're looking to buy a put option, what should you do?
    a. Buy the put option now
    b. Wait till the IV rank hits 80%
    c. Wait till the IV rank hits 50%
    d. Wait till the IV rank hits 70%
11. Which trading strategy is the best to use if you expect the stock to stay within a fixed range?
    a. Call Option
    b. Shorting a Stock
    c. Put Option
    d. Iron Condor
    e. Collar
12. Which trading strategy is the best to use if you expect the stock to crash?
    a. Call Option
    b. Shorting a Stock
    c. Put Option
    d. Iron Condor
    e. Collar
13. Which options strategy helps to reduce the cost of a put option?
    a. Call Option

b. Shorting a Stock
   c. Put Option
   d. Iron Condor
   e. Collar
14. Which options strategy is an alternative to buying a stock, which allows for less risk and more scale?
   a. Call Option
   b. Shorting a Stock
   c. Put Option
   d. Iron Condor
   e. Collar
15. Which is the most dangerous strategy in the stock market, which should be avoided?
   a. Call Option
   b. Shorting a Stock
   c. Put Option
   d. Iron Condor
   e. Collar

16. Jo buys 1 iron condor for Southern Copper stock that expires in 50 days. The two puts are at $40 and $45; and the two calls are at $70 and $75. Estimate the net premium received and draw a chart of price at expiration vs profit for the options contract.

| Trade | Select | ⓘ | 0 | 0 | 0.00 | 0 | 15.60 | 16.40 | 40.00 | 0.05 | 0.25 | 0.18 | 0 | 0 | 62 | ⓘ | Select | Trade |
|---|---|---|---|---|---|---|---|---|---|---|---|---|---|---|---|---|---|---|
| Trade | Select | ⓘ | 0 | 1 | 11.60 | 0 | 11.20 | 11.60 | 45.00 | 0.35 | 0.50 | 0.40 | 0 | 0 | 46 | ⓘ | Select | Trade |
| Trade | Select | ⓘ | 8 | 15 | 7.00 | -1.70 | 8.90 | 7.10 | 50.00 | 1.15 | 1.35 | 1.25 | +0.25 | 7 | 348 | ⓘ | Select | Trade |
| Trade | Select | ⓘ | 5 | 150 | 3.29 | -0.98 | 3.40 | 3.70 | 55.00 | 2.85 | 3.10 | 2.68 | +0.43 | 35 | 438 | ⓘ | Select | Trade |
| Trade | Select | ⓘ | 21 | 221 | 1.46 | -0.41 | 1.40 | 1.50 | 60.00 | 5.90 | 6.20 | 5.75 | +0.47 | 3 | 256 | ⓘ | Select | Trade |
| Trade | Select | ⓘ | 38 | 480 | 0.49 | -0.16 | 0.40 | 0.55 | 65.00 | 10.00 | 10.30 | 8.58 | 0 | 0 | 133 | ⓘ | Select | Trade |
| Trade | Select | ⓘ | 102 | 354 | 0.19 | -0.11 | 0.15 | 0.25 | 70.00 | 14.70 | 15.00 | 14.70 | +1.10 | 2 | 98 | ⓘ | Select | Trade |
| Trade | Select | ⓘ | 0 | 145 | 0.15 | 0 |  | 0.15 | 75.00 | 19.60 | 19.90 | 18.97 | 0 | 0 | 15 | ⓘ | Select | Trade |

Net Premium = ($15-$0)+($35-$5) = $45

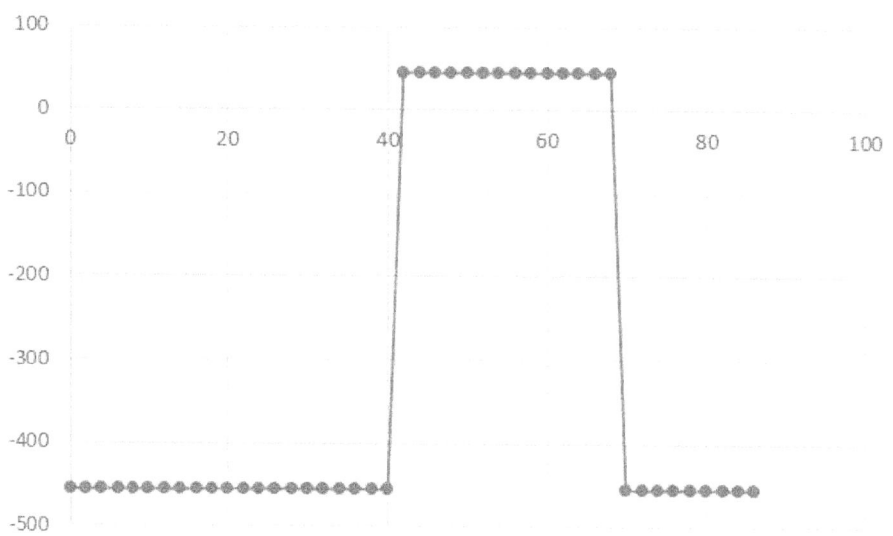

17. Cleo buys 1 iron condor for 3D systems stock that expires in 15 days. The two puts are at $20 and $22; and the two calls are at $32 and $34. Estimate the net premium received and draw a chart of price at expiration vs profit for the options contract.

Net Premium = ($35-$25)+($5-$0) = $15

| | | | | |
|---|---|---|---|---|
| 7.50 | 8.00 | 20.00 | 0.00 | 0.05 |
| 6.50 | 6.80 | 21.00 | 0.00 | 0.45 |
| 5.60 | 5.90 | 22.00 | 0.05 | 0.15 |
| 4.70 | 5.00 | 23.00 | 0.15 | 0.25 |
| 3.80 | 4.10 | 24.00 | 0.25 | 0.35 |
| 3.00 | 3.30 | 25.00 | 0.45 | 0.55 |
| 2.25 | 2.60 | 26.00 | 0.70 | 0.85 |
| 1.70 | 1.85 | 27.00 | 1.10 | 1.20 |
| 1.20 | 1.35 | 28.00 | 1.55 | 1.70 |
| 0.80 | 0.95 | 29.00 | 2.15 | 2.30 |
| 0.55 | 0.70 | 30.00 | 2.90 | 3.10 |
| 0.35 | 0.45 | 31.00 | 3.50 | 3.90 |
| 0.25 | 0.30 | 32.00 | 4.30 | 4.80 |

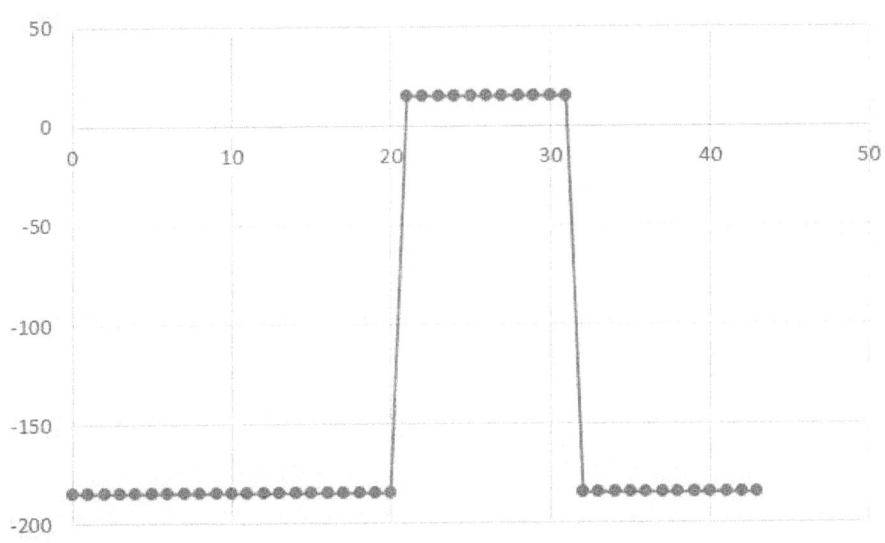

18. Bob sells 1 put option for Northern Star stock that expires in 141 days. The strike price is at $12.50. Estimate the net premium received and draw a chart of price at expiration vs profit for the options contract.

Net Premium = $220

19. Toby buys 1 call option for GLD stock that expires in 260 days. The strike price is at $170. Estimate the cost of the option and draw a chart of price at expiration vs profit for the options contract.

Cost of option = $625

20. Sam buys 1 put option for Ford stock that expires in 169 days. The strike price is at $12. Estimate the cost of the option and draw a chart of price at expiration vs profit for the options contract.

Cost of put option = $59

21. Tim buys 1 put option for Ford stock that expires in 196 days. The strike price is at $50. He then sells 1 call at $70 to offset the cost of the put.

    Estimate the cost of the option and draw a chart of price at expiration vs profit for the options contract.

Cost of collar = $160-$640 = -$480 (Tim receives a net premium of $480)

| | | | | |
|---|---|---|---|---|
| 17.40 | 18.70 | 50.00 | 1.60 | 2.15 |
| 13.20 | 14.20 | 55.00 | 2.70 | 3.40 |
| 10.50 | 13.80 | 57.50 | 3.60 | 4.10 |
| 9.40 | 10.50 | 60.00 | 4.50 | 5.30 |
| 7.90 | 8.60 | 62.50 | 5.60 | 6.40 |
| 6.40 | 6.90 | 65.00 | 6.90 | 7.80 |

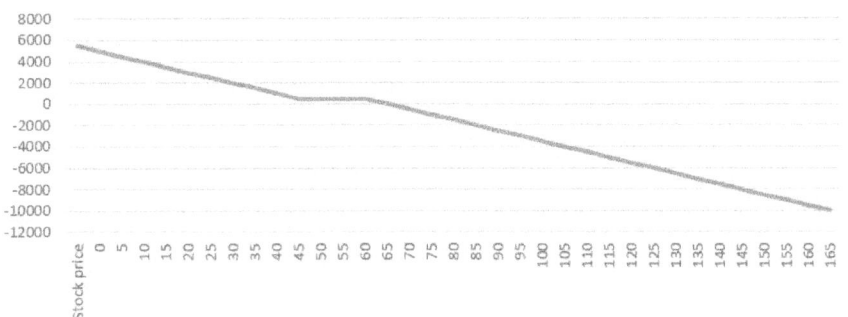

Profit per contract

22. Kandy buys 1 put option for Ark investment stock that expires in 113 days. The strike price is at $100. He then sells 1 call at $110 to offset the cost of the put.
   Estimate the cost of the option and draw a chart of price at expiration vs profit for the options contract.

Cost of collar = $570 - $865 = -$295 (Kandy receives $295 as a premium)

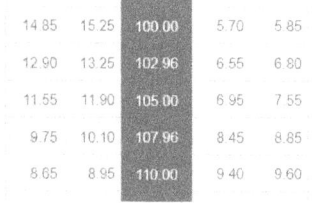

| | | | | |
|---|---|---|---|---|
| 14.85 | 15.25 | 100.00 | 5.70 | 5.85 |
| 12.90 | 13.25 | 102.96 | 6.55 | 6.80 |
| 11.55 | 11.90 | 105.00 | 6.95 | 7.55 |
| 9.75 | 10.10 | 107.96 | 8.45 | 8.85 |
| 8.65 | 8.95 | 110.00 | 9.40 | 9.60 |

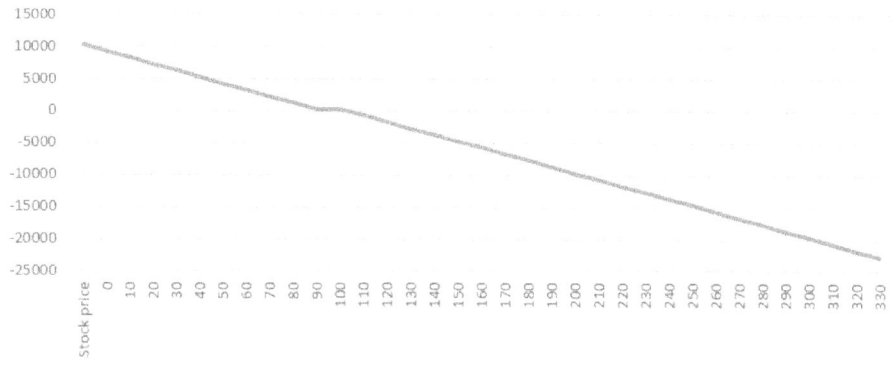

23. Sammy buys a collar for EDU stock; with the put price at $1.5 and the call at $2.

   Estimate the cost of the option and draw a chart of price at expiration vs profit for the options contract.

Cost of collar = $15 - $40 = -$25 (Sammy receives $25 as premium)

| 0.65 | 0.80 | 1.50 | 0.15 | 0.25 |
|------|------|------|------|------|
| 0.40 | 0.55 | 2.00 | 0.40 | 0.50 |

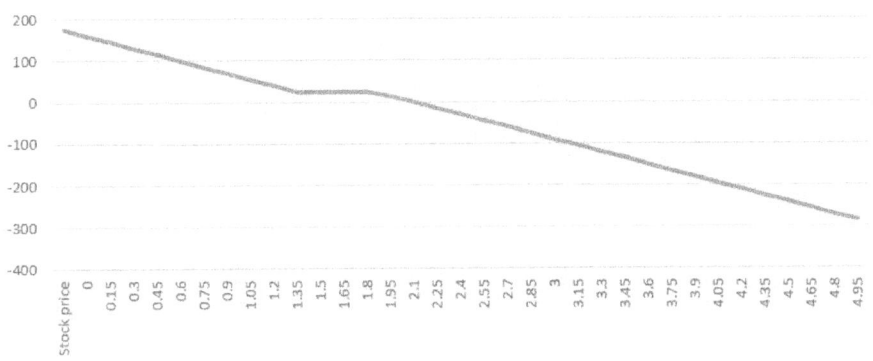

24. Elona buys a put option for Tesla stock; with the strike price at $750. Estimate the cost of the option and draw a chart of price at expiration vs profit for the options contract.

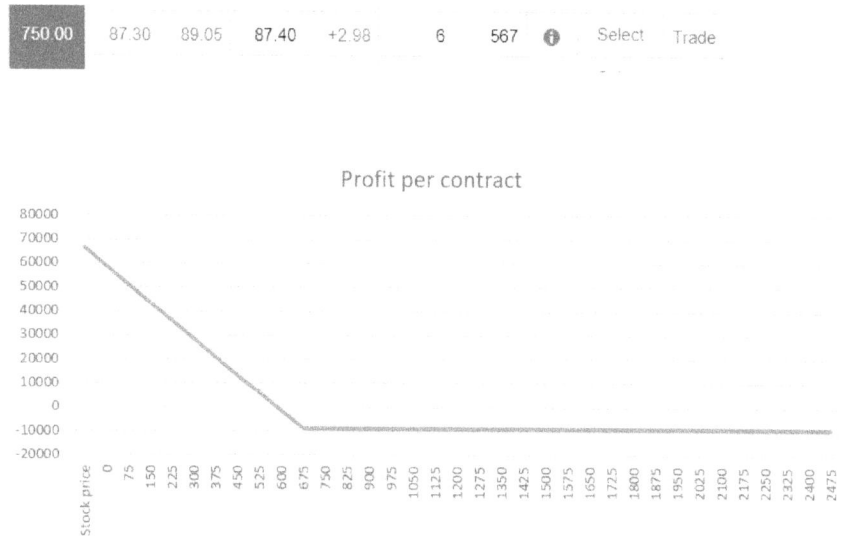

25. Fiona buys a put option for Microsoft stock; with the strike price at $250.

   Estimate the cost of the option and draw a chart of price at expiration vs profit for the options contract.

Cost of put = $930

| 250.00 | 9.30 | 13.80 | 11.20 | +0.90 |

Profit per contract

26. Bob purchases an Iron Condor for Advanced Micro Devices (AMD) that expires in 77 days.

The put strike prices are $85 and $90; while the call strike prices are $135 and $140.

   a. What is the net premium he receives?
   b. What happens if AMD expires at $150?
   c. What happens if AMD expires at $125?
   d. What happens if AMD expires at $80?
   e. What happens if AMD expires at $136?

<br>

a. Net Premium for puts = $104
   Net Premium for calls = $24
   Net Premium received = $104 + $24 = $128
b. Profit on $140 call = $1000
   Loss on $135 call = $1500
   Net loss = $1500 - $1000 - $128 Loss = **$372 Loss**
c. Profit = Net Premium = $128
d. **$372 Loss**
e. **$272 Profit**

27. William owns 100 shares of Toyota Motors. He sells a collar; buying a put at $160 and selling a call at $165. It expires in 112 days.

    a. Cost of Put = $220
        Premium for Call = $1590
        Cost of Put = - $1370. William gets paid for the collar
   b. Profit = $1370 + $1000 = $2370
   c. Profit of $870

Assume that the minimum prices are paid for buying/selling puts/calls

28. Tim owns 100 shares of Intel stock, and he wants to complete a vertical spread where he sells a call option at $50 and buy a call option at $55.

- How many contracts can he sell?
- What is the net premium that he receives?
- What happens if Intel stock is at $70 at expiration?
- What happens if Intel stock is at $30 at expiration?

- 1 contract
- $0
- Loss of $500
- No gain or loss

29. You sell 1 put option of Electronic Arts below.
    - When's the expiration date of the options above?
    - What is the premium you would receive for selling 1 put option at a strike price of $120? Assume that you get paid the minimum amount in the range.
    - How much cash do you need as collateral to sell 1 put option at a strike price of $120?
    - What happens if EA stock is at $160 after 112 days?
    - What happens if EA stock is at $90 after 112 days?



- January 21, 2022
- $240
- $120000
- Profit of $240
- Got to sell stock at strike price of $120. Resulting **loss of $2760**.

30. Jack buys 2 contracts of Twitter call options that expire in 168 days. The strike price for the contract is **$65**. Assume that Jack pays the minimum required premium for the stock.

If the Twitter price in 168 days is $100:

- How many shares of stock does Jack have the option to buy?
- How much premium does Jack pay for the contract? (Assume that Alice pays the minimum amount)
- How much profit does Jack make in 168 days?


- 200 shares
- $575*2 = **$1150**
- **$2350 profit**

www.ingramcontent.com/pod-product-compliance
Lightning Source LLC
Chambersburg PA
CBHW071608080526
44588CB00010B/1063